SpringerBriefs in Information Systems

Series Editor

Jörg Becker, Münster, Germany

SpringerBriefs present concise summaries of cutting-edge research and practical applications across a wide spectrum of fields. Featuring compact volumes of 50 to 125 pages, the series covers a range of content from professional to academic. Typical topics might include: A timely report of state-of-the art analytical techniques, a bridge between new research results, as published in journal articles, and a contextual literature review, a snapshot of a hot or emerging topic, an in-depth case study or practical example, a presentation of core concepts that students must understand in order to make independent contributions. SpringerBriefs in Information Systems showcase emerging theory, empirical research, and practical application in all subcategories of information systems and related fields, from a global author community. Briefs are characterized by fast, global electronic dissemination, standard publishing contracts, standardized manuscript preparation and formatting guidelines, and expedited production schedules

More information about this series at http://www.springer.com/series/10189

Christian Hovestadt • Jan Recker • Janek Richter •
Karl Werder
Editors

Digital Responses to Covid-19

Digital Innovation, Transformation, and Entrepreneurship During Pandemic Outbreaks

Springer

Editors
Christian Hovestadt
University of Cologne
Cologne, Germany

Jan Recker
University of Cologne
Cologne, Germany

Janek Richter
University of Cologne
Cologne, Germany

Karl Werder
University of Cologne
Cologne, Germany

ISSN 2192-4929 ISSN 2192-4937 (electronic)
SpringerBriefs in Information Systems
ISBN 978-3-030-66610-1 ISBN 978-3-030-66611-8 (eBook)
https://doi.org/10.1007/978-3-030-66611-8

This Springer imprint is published by the registered company Springer Nature Switzerland AG.
The registered company address is: Gewerbestrasse 11, 6330 Cham, Switzerland

Preface

Can information systems help save the planet? This has been a question pestering information systems researchers for years. In 2020, when the COVID-19 outbreak began affecting the entire planet, the question became not only more pressing but urgent.

In our own teaching, we explored this question whilst being impacted by the crisis. Together with master's students in information systems at the University of Cologne, we reviewed, discussed, explored, and ideated how information systems can help during the pandemic and after. We settled on what we now call digital responses to COVID-19—solutions in the form of digital innovations, digital transformations, and digital entrepreneurship that help individuals, collectives, businesses, and society at large to understand the crisis, mitigate its negative impact, and leverage its potential opportunities.

After the course had finished in July 2020, we wanted to take our learnings outside of the (virtual) classroom and into society. We felt that our jointly developed knowledge and ideas can perhaps be a small stepping stone for businesses that are struggling, sectors that need inspiration, and society that needs to come to terms with the pandemic. So we decided to continue to work on the ideas, well beyond the point where students were graded for their efforts, and make their work and outcomes available to the public.

This book is the outcome of this effort. Together with our students, we continued to refine and revise the ideas, culminating in a set of nine essays, an introduction, and a conclusion. We are not idealists; we know that this book is not solving the challenges the pandemic brings. But it contains a wealth of analyses, insights, ideas, and concepts that are now available for others to inspect, reflect, criticize, or develop further. Incrementally, this knowledge will allow others to add new knowledge, find more effective solutions, and—step by step—allow us to solve this global crisis, and prepare for the next, whatever form it may take.

We thank our students for investing their time and effort not only in the classroom from April to July 2020 but beyond. We hope you, as a reader, will receive some inspiration, some ideas, and some opportunity for reflection from the many good ideas the essays contain.

Happy reading. Stay safe, and well.

Cologne, Germany
November 2020

Christian Hovestadt
Jan Recker
Janek Richter
Karl Werder

Contents

Contributors

Sefa Basar University of Cologne, Cologne, Germany

Shanice Casado Gracia University of Cologne, Cologne, Germany

Jana Feldkamp University of Cologne, Cologne, Germany

Fritz Hädrich University of Cologne, Cologne, Germany

Christian Hovestadt University of Cologne, Cologne, Germany

Lorenz Kriehn University of Cologne, Cologne, Germany

Simon Murillo University of Cologne, Cologne, Germany

Jan Recker University of Cologne, Cologne, Germany

Janek Richter University of Cologne, Cologne, Germany

Zacharias Schrage University of Cologne, Cologne, Germany

Jana Teutenberg University of Cologne, Cologne, Germany

Ivan Trilevic University of Cologne, Cologne, Germany

Karl Werder University of Cologne, Cologne, Germany

Chapter 1
Introduction

Christian Hovestadt, Jan Recker, Janek Richter, and Karl Werder

Abstract The COVID-19 pandemic has forced society and individuals to change their behavior in many drastic ways. Responses to this new reality can be digitally enabled. We propose three important dimensions that help us to classify digitally enabled responses: class of response, type of knowledge contribution, and level of analysis. This threefold perspective helps us position the contributions of the following nine chapters in this book.

Keywords Digital responses · COVID-19 pandemic · Digital innovation · Digital entrepreneurship · Digital transformation

The Response to COVID-19 Is Digitally Enabled

The COVID-19 pandemic has changed our world forever. Millions of people have been infected and hundreds of thousands of people have died. Most countries have implemented strict lockdowns, social life has waned, cultural and artist experiences have suffered. Education of children and students had to move online, and many businesses may not survive.

At the time of writing this introductory chapter in October 2020, more than 40 million cases of COVID-19 have been reported with over one million deaths. Most cases and deaths have been reported in the United States, yet infection and death rates in other countries, such as India, Brazil, and Russia, are also rising rapidly. Europe is in the middle of a second wave of infections, in many places with worse trajectories than during the first wave between March and June 2020. These numbers are staggering and the developments they indicate concerning.

The outbreak and evolution of the pandemic has put science squarely into the spotlight of society. The involvement of scientists in discussions of large-scale

---

C. Hovestadt · J. Recker (✉) · J. Richter · K. Werder
University of Cologne, Cologne, Germany
e-mail: hovestadt@wiso.uni-koeln.de; jan.recker@wiso.uni-koeln.de; janek.richter@wiso.uni-koeln.de; werder@wiso.uni-koeln.de

C. Hovestadt et al. (eds.), *Digital Responses to Covid-19*, SpringerBriefs in Information Systems, https://doi.org/10.1007/978-3-030-66611-8_1

political, societal, or economical countermeasures has been intensely debated, either because they have been, or because they have not been, involved in the development or implementation of such measures. The scientific community has also responded on its own. Scholars around the world are working hard in a synchronized and concerted effort to find a vaccine against COVID-19 (R&D Blue Print 2020). Research data and publications are being made open and shared at an unprecedented pace and volume (e.g., Springer Nature 2020), hoping to accelerate the development of vaccines, medications, and other interventions that can pause if not halt the pandemic, or mitigate if not eradicate its impact on the economy or societies at large.

As scholars in many disciplines around the world are collaborating in this so-called "war" to fight the virus and its many consequences, the question begs whether and in what form information systems (IS) scholars can contribute to this global effort (Ågerfalk et al. 2020; Thomas et al. 2020). While IS scholars might not be able to develop a vaccine or help understand virological or epidemiological properties and developments, they possess an excellent theoretical and methodical repertoire to understand how digital technologies, that is, electronic tools, systems, devices and resources that generate, store, or process data (Fichman et al. 2014), can be used to foster and enhance the resilience of people, communities and organisations by strengthening their ability to adapt to uncertainty, enabling a transition towards an appropriate restoration of order in society (Rai 2020; Sakurai and Chughtai 2020).

Responding to COVID-19 and building resilience draws on digitally enabled efforts of innovation, transformation, and entrepreneurship, all of which seem more necessary than ever (Baig et al. 2020). The COVID-19 crisis produced profound and impactful environmental changes through geospatial restrictions (e.g., air travel), political measures (e.g., bans of large social gatherings) and sociodemographic changes (e.g., counter-movements and protests) (Davidsson et al. 2020). COVID-19 triggered sudden demand shifts (e.g., for face masks but also for storable household goods like toilet paper and canned food), it shifted structures and processes in organizations (e.g., by forcing a workforce to work remotely), it created a need to substitute suddenly scarce resources (e.g., because global supply chains broke down), and it led to the development of entirely novel offerings, such as decision support systems that display crowding information (e.g., how crowded a medical practice is) to encourage physical distancing when users select locations (Adam et al. 2020). Incumbent organizations drew on digital technology to facilitate and support work under COVID-19 restrictions, such as collaborating from home (Waizenegger et al. 2020). Others have used digital technology such as 3D-printing systems to adapt their manufacturing processes and produce items in sudden global demand such as face masks or oxygen valves (Petch 2020).

But not only is digital technology at the heart of changes evoked through the crisis or launched in response. The pandemic itself presents an IS challenge. One of the first realizations about COVID-19 was that it created an epidemic as well as an *infodemic*, as large amounts of misinformation spread through social media and other information channels (Laato et al. 2020). Different kinds of IS solutions have been developed and used during the COVID-19 pandemic (Abeler et al. 2020; Calvo et al. 2020; Dong et al. 2020). For example, the COVID-19 pandemic has created a need for rapid, population-wide digital contact tracing (Riemer et al. 2020). Moreover, policy makers (Lazzerini and Putoto 2020), health professionals (Reeves et al. 2020), and billions of citizens worldwide (Stafford 2020) frequent COVID-19 dashboards that track the outbreak and trajectory of the virus across time and geographical regions (Dong et al. 2020; Donovan 2020). The COVID-19-Dashboard by the German federal health research institute (Robert-Koch-Institut (RKI)) (https://corona.rki.de), the Johns Hopkins University's COVID-19 Global Map in the US (https://coronavirus.jhu.edu/map.html), or the World Health Organization's Coronavirus Disease (COVID-19) Dashboard (https://covid19.who.int/) are prominent examples.

The world is looking for help and it looks in particular at digital technologies to help them understand the crisis and mitigate its consequences. From the beginning of the pandemic outbreak, gathering, analyzing, interpreting, and disseminating information as well as determining the value of technological solutions have been of crucial importance (Calvo et al. 2020; Dong et al. 2020). IS solutions can help to better understand the crisis and its spread through "track and trace" data about the pandemic (Abeler et al. 2020). Many countries have developed contact tracing applications that notify people in case they were physically exposed to infected COVID-19 patients (Trang et al. 2020). In Germany, its voluntary use, reliance on anonymous data, privacy protection, and open source nature, led to more than 18 million downloads within 100 days of its release. Similarly, COVID-19 dashboards have been helpful in order to understand the spread of the pandemic and understand the consequences of policy changes. The COVID-19 dashboard (Donovan 2020) by John Hopkins University in the US has been used by billions of people globally as an informational source aggregating multiple data streams into a single cockpit. Monthly visits to Germany's RKI COVID-19-Dashboard increased from 630,000 (December 2019) and 1,700,000 (January 2020) to 6,200,000 (February 2020) and a staggering 66,600,000 visitors in March 2020 (SimilarWeb 2020). Digital technologies also help people to mitigate the consequences of the crisis. Video conferencing services have been increasingly adopted in order mitigate social disconnect between coworkers during lockdowns and physical distancing guidelines (Hacker et al. 2020). As a result, *Zoom*, a video conferencing service provider, has quadrupled its revenue because of a surge in demand of their solution (Chapman 2020). Such digital technologies help businesses and schools to facilitate remote collaboration and virtual education.

Using This Book to Identify Digital Responses to COVID-19

In this book, we present nine essays that explore possible contributions IS scholars can make toward managing businesses during a global pandemic. These essays stem from a post-graduate course on "Selected Issues in Information Systems", held in the summer term 2020 by the Cologne Institute of Information Systems at the University of Cologne. This course was originally designed to focus on issues with IS that had nothing to do with COVID-19. However, as the lockdown occurred in March 2020 and university regulations affecting physical presence education and course design were changed in the following weeks, a decision was made not only to change the mode of teaching but also the content. In a course exploring issues with digitalization, which had to be offered entirely through digital means, why not use the opportunity to explore how digitalization could be used to respond to the unfolding pandemic?

To prepare students for their essays on how digital responses to COVID-19 might look like, the course started with in-depth presentations, reviews, and discussions of the latest theoretical and empirical knowledge in IS research about four topic areas:

1. Digital technologies (Ekbia 2009; Faulkner and Runde 2019; Jarvenpaa and Standaert 2018; Tilson et al. 2010): new theory or new empirical findings about digital artifacts, such as apps, devices, infrastructures, platforms, dashboards, or other objects.
2. Digital innovations (Bragge et al. 2011; Kyriakou et al. 2017; Lee and Berente 2012; Lyytinen et al. 2016; Svahn et al. 2017): new theory or new empirical findings about the management of new product or service offerings embodied in or enabled by information and communication technology.
3. Digital transformations (Gregory et al. 2018; Henfridsson et al. 2014; Sebastian et al. 2017; Selander and Jarvenpaa 2016): new theory or new empirical findings about incumbent organizations' technology-enabled changes to offerings, business models, structures, or processes.
4. Digital entrepreneurship (Nambisan and Baron 2021; Tumbas et al. 2018; von Briel et al. 2018a, b): new theory or new empirical findings about the emergence of new digital ventures.

Students had to read papers, watch video lectures, and present their critical reflections on those papers. Their understanding of the fundamental papers was assessed through a comprehension online quiz, while live online sessions were used for discussion and debate of content and implications.

Having laid out the conceptual and empirical foundation, students then had to develop their own ideas. They were tasked to explore how digital technologies, innovation, transformation, or entrepreneurship can help during pandemics such as the COVID-19 crisis. They were free to pick a topic of their own choosing. To guide them in the selection process, three types of phenomena were discussed that were prevalent at that time (May 2020).

1. At that time, in the media, a discourse was ongoing about individual and organizational responses in terms of new or changed digital practices: how does home schooling work? How could childcare facilities offer support through digital technologies to children that cannot yet read or write? How can the hospitality and tourism sector recover and sustain itself? What are the issues surrounding the development and use of a contact tracing app and how could they

be solved? Which businesses do well during the pandemic and why? How could traditional, non-digital companies prepare for the post-Corona world?
2. Many of the students had themselves experienced or learned about new digital phenomena that emerged together with the unfolding pandemic: For example, students asked themselves which digital start-ups they had seen emerge during the pandemic and what their core digital value propositions were. They asked, will these ventures be successful in a post-Corona world?
3. During the online discussions, students also engaged in critical appraisals about issues they witnessed or experienced during the lockdown that were implemented in Germany at that time. Questions they explored included: What are the short- and potential long-term impacts of newly developed digital technologies on people, organizations, and society? For example, are the Corona dashboards by the RKI or the John Hopkins University truly informing the population or are they susceptible to misinformation? What is the role of "fake news" and internet trolls during the pandemic? Will short-term fixes (e.g., monitoring of infected people via an app) lead to a permanent state of surveillance? As individuals, organizations and governments are being forced to make quick decisions with far-reaching consequences, what are the longer-term societal implications of these decisions and their resultant digital solutions and practices?

With these three pillars of inspiration provided, students were free to develop conceptual, empirical, or design-oriented contributions. This was important because IS research embraces pluralism and is open to any tradition that advances existing theories or generates new theoretical lenses (Rai 2018). Over the progression of the course, the students formulated and developed their ideas in the form of seminar papers. After the course had finished, these papers underwent two rounds of review and revision managed by the editors of this book, ultimately culminating in the chapters presented in this volume. In sum, the students explored content choices alongside three dimensions:

1. The paper's focus on one of three classes of digitally enabled responses to COVID-19:
   - digital innovation (i.e., a new ICT-enabled product or service offering),
   - digital transformation (i.e., an incumbent organization's technology-enabled change because of the pandemic), or
   - digital entrepreneurship (i.e., the emergence of a new digital venture).
2. The paper's type of knowledge contribution given the chosen focus:
   - empirical (e.g., a case study of a new technology, a novel innovation, an organization transforming, or a new startup emerging),
   - conceptual (e.g., a review of which theoretical concepts from the literature on digital technologies, innovation, transformation, or entrepreneurship could inform actions in the crisis that could be taken by society, government, companies, or citizens), or
   - design-oriented (e.g., a new concept for a software system that helps monitoring of infected people via an app).

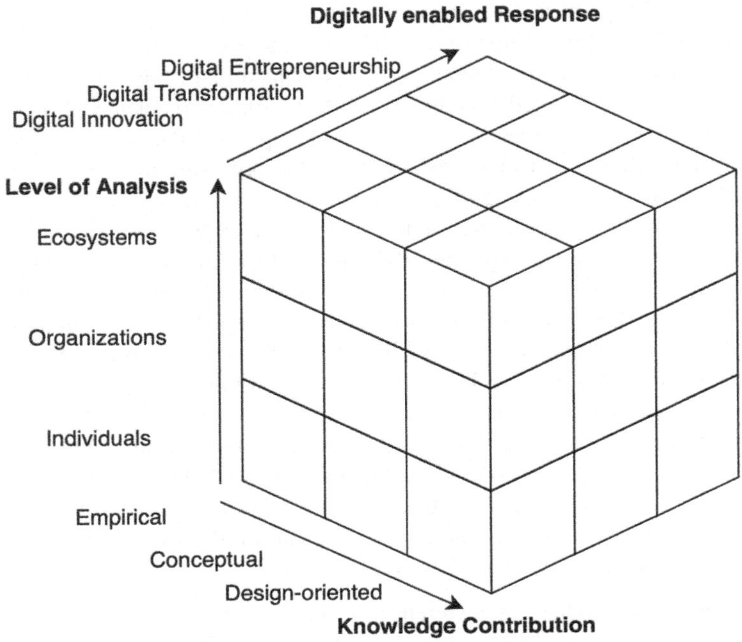

Fig. 1.1 A framework to position research on digital responses to COVID-19

3. The paper's level of analysis (i.e., the target audience that the paper speaks to):
   - individuals or particular groups of individuals (e.g., all citizens, all policy makers, all infected people, all immunized people, all students, all organizational staff),
   - organizations (e.g., firms, universities, schools), or
   - ecosystems and society (e.g., countries, industry sectors).

As such, this book covers contributions about how a digital response to COVID-19 might manifest, across a three-dimensional space (Fig. 1.1): by class of digitally enabled solutions for handling the pandemic, by type of knowledge contribution sought, and by level of analysis. While there have been many calls for IS research to address challenges from and develop solutions for implications of the COVID-19 pandemic (Ågerfalk et al. 2020; Rai 2020; Thomas et al. 2020), there has not been a curated edited volume that combines such a varied and broad spectrum of contributions exemplary of the type of solutions that IS scholars can help develop.

We present how each of the chapters relates to the three dimensions. First, the book presents **three different types of digitally enabled solutions** for handling the pandemic. Chapters 2–4 present different examples of digital innovation—that is, new product or service offerings enabled by digital technology—that help managing the pandemic. Chapters 5–7 present three examples of digital transformation—that

Table 1.1 Overview of papers

Chapter, author	Digitally-enabled response	Level of analysis	Knowledge contribution
2. Hädrich	Digital innovation	Individual	Empirical
3. Kriehn	Digital innovation	Ecosystem/ society	Empirical
4. Trilevic	Digital innovation	Organization	Design-oriented
5. Murillo	Digital transformation	Individuals	Conceptual, design-oriented
6. Feldkamp	Digital transformation	Ecosystem	Conceptual
7. Schrage	Digital transformation	Organization	Conceptual
8. Teutenberg	Digital entrepreneurship	Organization	Empirical
9. Gracia	Digital entrepreneurship	Organization	Design-oriented
10. Basar	Digital entrepreneurship	Organization	Design-oriented

is, incumbent organization's technology-enabled change—by exploring the transformative role of the global pandemic as a trigger to change. Chapters 8–10 present three cases of digital entrepreneurship—that is, the emergence of a new digital venture.

With these distinctions, the chapters also provide different temporal perspectives on the pandemic. Chapters 2–4 focuses on digital innovations whose developments have been accelerated by the pandemic. In Chaps. 5–7, on-going change processes about how to cope with the pandemic are being investigated. Chapters 8–10 take a forward looking-perspective and focus on emergent opportunities that can be seized immediately by entrepreneurs over the course of the pandemic.

Second, the book provides **three different types of knowledge contributions** across the individual chapters: Empirical, conceptual, and design-oriented. For example, Chap. 3 presents an empirical investigation of the contact tracing app commissioned and launched by the German government. Chapter 7 reviews software development control practices and conceptualizes how software development teams need to adapt as they are forced to work remotely from home during the global pandemic. Chapter 10 develops and designs a concept for a digital restaurant system that relies on an entirely digitized ordering and payment process to minimize the risk of infection for customers and personnel.

Third, the essays in this book also provide contributions on **three different levels of analysis**: individuals and groups, organizations, and ecosystems. To illustrate, Chap. 5 discusses how digital tools can help improve individuals learning during COVID-19. In Chap. 8, a digital venture in the event business is reviewed, which exploited its digital competencies to emerge successful from the crisis. Chapter 6 investigates the societal rise of TikTok—a social media platform.

Table 1.1 summarizes the contributions included in this book and how they are positioned within the three-dimensional space outlined in Fig. 1.1. Fritz Hädrich investigated popular COVID-19 dashboards and their tracking abilities. Lorenz Kriehn reviewed the Corona tracing app launched by the German government and its development process. Ivan Trilevic proposed a new concept for an online platform for offering courses in support of children's development. Simon Friedrich

Murillo explored how digital tools can support young people's learning in times of a global pandemic. The evolution of TikTok as one of the most popular social media platforms among young adults was the subject of investigation by Jana Feldkamp. Zacharias Schrage reviewed the literature on control practices in software development in order to propose adjustments needed to those practices in times of the COVID-19 pandemic. Jana Teutenberg investigated how a new digital venture identified a new opportunity for a digital business model during the COVID-19 pandemic and how this affected the transformation of their business model. Shanice Casado Gracia developed an application concept that provides pandemic control measures for grocery stores. Sefa Basar developed a software concept for an ordering system that minimizes the risk exposure of customers and waiters in restaurants.

While we do not assert that the three dimensions used to position the essays in this book comprehensively cover all the ways in which IS scholars can contribute to responses to the COVID-19 pandemic, we see it as a suitable way to evaluate the space in which COVID-19 problems or digitally enabled responses as solutions might manifest. Empty cells in our multidimensional space might indicate a need for new solutions. Cells filled with several contributions might be seen as appropriately responded to. As the COVID-19 pandemic progresses and evolves over time, IS scholars will need to constantly revisit, evaluate, and further develop contributions to responses. Our framework might enable us to critically reflect about whether we see the pandemic or the potential solution space as fruitful and effective paths forward. We hope the contributions developed by our IS students serve both as illumination and inspiration to that end. Although we supervised, guided, reviewed, and helped revise their work, we felt it was important to keep the ideas and voice of the students as original as possible. This book covers their ideas and we want to acknowledge the effort our students have put into their tasks well beyond the boundaries of the class (or any grading criteria). We hope this book illustrates the contributions we all can make as we start to think about how IS scholarship can play a small but substantial role in handling what appears to be one of the biggest global societal challenges of our time. We were inspired by our students' ideas and we hope this book conveys the same message.

References

Abeler, J., Bäcker, M., Buermeyer, U., & Zillessen, H. (2020). COVID-19 contact tracing and data protection can go together. *JMIR Mhealth Uhealth, 8*(4), e19359. https://doi.org/10.2196/19359.

Adam, M., Werner, D., Wendt, C., & Benlian, A. (2020). Containing COVID-19 through physical distancing: The impact of real-time crowding information. *European Journal of Information Systems, 1*, 13. https://doi.org/10.1080/0960085X.2020.1814681.

Ågerfalk, P. J., Conboy, K., & Myers, M. D. (2020). Information systems in the age of pandemics: COVID-19 and beyond. *European Journal of Information Systems, 29*(3), 203–207. https://doi.org/10.1080/0960085X.2020.1771968.

Baig, A., Hall, B., Jenkins, P., Lamarre, E., & McCarthy, B. (2020). *The COVID-19 recovery will be digital: A plan for the first 90 days*. McKInsey. Retrieved June 29.

Bragge, J., Tuunanen, T., Virtanen, V., & Svahn, S. (2011). Designing a repeatable collaboration method for setting up emerging value systems for new technology fields. *Journal of Information Technology Theory and Application, 12*(3), 27–47.

Calvo, R. A., Deterding, S., & Ryan, R. M. (2020). Health surveillance during Covid-19 pandemic. *British Medical Journal, 369*. https://doi.org/10.1136/bmj.m1373

Chapman, B. (2020). Zoom's revenues quadruple as pandemic causes huge surge in video conferencing. *The Independent*. Retrieved November 9, from https://www.independent.co.uk/news/business/news/zoom-results-sales-rise-coronavirus-pandemic-video-conferencing-a9698086.html

Davidsson, P., Recker, J., & von Briel, F. (2020). External enablement of new venture creation: A framework. *Academy of Management Perspectives, 34*(3), 311–332. https://doi.org/10.5465/amp.2017.0163.

Dong, E., Du, H., & Gardner, L. (2020). An interactive web-based dashboard to track COVID-19 in real time. *The Lancet, 20*(5), 533–534

Donovan, D. (2020). *Map tracks coronavirus outbreak in near real time*. Johns Hopkins University. Retrieved May 12, from https://hub.jhu.edu/2020/01/23/coronavirus-outbreak-mapping-tool-649-em1-art1-dtd-health/

Ekbia, H. R. (2009). Digital artifacts as quasi-objects: Qualification, mediation, and materiality. *Journal of the American Society for Information Science and Technology, 60*(12), 2554–2566.

Faulkner, P., & Runde, J. (2019). Theorizing the digital object. *MIS Quarterly, 43*(4), 1279–1302.

Fichman, R. G., Dos Santos, B. L., & Zheng, Z. (2014). Digital innovation as a fundamental and powerful concept in the information systems curriculum. *MIS Quarterly, 38*(2), 329–353.

Gregory, R. W., Kaganer, E., Henfridsson, O., & Ruch, T. J. (2018). IT consumerization and the transformation of IT governance. *MIS Quarterly, 42*(4), 1225–1253.

Hacker, J., vom Brocke, J., Handali, J., Otto, M., & Schneider, J. (2020). Virtually in this together – How web-conferencing systems enabled a new virtual togetherness during the COVID-19 crisis. *European Journal of Information Systems, 1*, 22. https://doi.org/10.1080/0960085X.2020.1814680.

Henfridsson, O., Mathiassen, L., & Svahn, F. (2014). Managing technological change in the digital age: The role of architectural frames. *Journal of Information Technology, 29*(1), 27–43.

Jarvenpaa, S. L., & Standaert, W. (2018). Digital probes as opening possibilities of generativity. *Journal of the Association for Information Systems, 19*(10), 982–1000.

Kyriakou, H., Nickerson, J. V., & Sabnis, G. (2017). Knowledge reuse for customization: Metamodels in an open design community for 3D printing. *MIS Quarterly, 41*(1), 315–332.

Laato, S., Najmul Islam, A. K. M., Nazrul Islam, M., & Whelan, E. (2020). What drives unverified information sharing and cyberchondria during the COVID-19 pandemic? *European Journal of Information Systems, 29*(3), 288–305. https://doi.org/10.1080/0960085X.2020.1770632.

Lazzerini, M., & Putoto, G. (2020). COVID-19 in Italy: Momentous decisions and many uncertainties. *Lancet, 8*(5), E641–E642.

Lee, J., & Berente, N. (2012). Digital innovation and the division of innovative labor: Digital controls in the automotive industry. *Organization Science, 23*(5), 1428–1447.

Lyytinen, K., Yoo, Y., & Boland, R. J. (2016). Digital product innovation within four classes of innovation networks. *Information Systems Journal, 26*(1), 47–75.

Nambisan, S., & Baron, R. (2021). On the costs of digital entrepreneurship: Role conflict, stress, and venture performance in digital platform-based ecosystems. *Journal of Business Research*. https://doi.org/10.1016/j.jbusres.2019.06.037.

Petch, M. (2020). *3D printing community responds to COVID-19 and coronavirus resources*. 3DPI. Retrieved October 7, from https://3dprintingindustry.com/news/3d-printing-community-responds-to-covid-19-and-coronavirus-resources-169143/

R&D Blue Print. (2020). *DRAFT landscape of COVID-19 candidate vaccines – 3 November2020*. World Health Organization. Retrieved November 9, from https://www.who.int/publications/m/item/draft-landscape-of-covid-19-candidate-vaccines

Rai, A. (2018). Editor's comments: beyond outdated labels: The blending of IS research traditions. *MIS Quarterly, 42*(1), iii–vi.

Rai, A. (2020). Editor's comments: The COVID-19 pandemic: Building resilience with IS research. *MIS Quarterly, 44*(2), iii–vii.

Reeves, J. J., Hollandsworth, H. M., Torriani, F. J., Taplitz, R., Abeles, S., Tai-Seale, M., Millen, M., Clay, B. J., & Longhurst, C. A. (2020). Rapid response to COVID-19: Health informatics support for outbreak management in an academic health system. *Journal of the American Medical Informatics Association, 27*, 853–859. https://doi.org/10.1093/jamia/ocaa037.

Riemer, K., Ciriello, R., Peter, S., & Schlagwein, D. (2020). Digital contact-tracing adoption in the COVID-19 pandemic: IT governance for collective action at the societal level. *European Journal of Information Systems, 1*, 15. https://doi.org/10.1080/0960085X.2020.1819898.

Sakurai, M., & Chughtai, H. (2020). Resilience against crises: COVID-19 and lessons from natural disasters. *European Journal of Information Systems, 1*, 10. https://doi.org/10.1080/0960085X.2020.1814171.

Sebastian, I. M., Ross, J. W., Beath, C. M., Mocker, M., Moloney, K. G., & Fonstad, N. O. (2017). How big old companies navigate digital transformation. *MIS Quarterly Executive, 16*(3), 197–213.

Selander, L., & Jarvenpaa, S. L. (2016). Digital action repertoires and transforming a social movement organization. *MIS Quarterly, 40*(2), 331–352.

SimilarWeb. (2020). *Traffic overview,* Mar 2020. SimilarWeb. Retrieved April 5, from https://www.similarweb.com/website/rki.de#overview

Springer Nature. (2020). *Research data support service for COVID-19 data*. Springer. Retrieved April 20, from https://www.springernature.com/de/researchers/campaigns/coronavirus/research-data

Stafford, N. (2020). Covid-19: Why Germany's case fatality rate seems so low. *British Medical Journal, 369*, m1395. https://doi.org/10.1136/bmj.m1395.

Svahn, F., Mathiassen, L., & Lindgren, R. (2017). Embracing digital innovation in incumbent firms: How Volvo cars managed competing concerns. *MIS Quarterly, 41*(1), 239–253.

Thomas, O., Hagen, S., Frank, U., Recker, J., Wessel, L., Kammler, F., Zarvic, & Timm, I. (2020). Global crises and the role of BISE. *Business & Information Systems Engineering, 62*(4), 385–396. https://doi.org/10.1007/s12599-020-00657-w.

Tilson, D., Lyytinen, K., & Sørensen, C. (2010). Digital infrastructures: The missing IS research agenda. *Information Systems Research, 21*(4), 748–459.

Trang, S., Trenz, M., Weiger, W. H., Tarafdar, M., & Cheung, C. M. K. (2020). One app to trace them all? Examining app specifications for mass acceptance of contact-tracing apps. *European Journal of Information Systems, 29*, 415–428. https://doi.org/10.1080/0960085X.2020.1784046.

Tumbas, S., Berente, N., & vom Brocke, J. (2018). Digital innovation and institutional entrepreneurship: Chief digital officer perspectives of their emerging role. *Journal of Information Technology, 33*(3), 188–202.

von Briel, F., Davidsson, P., & Recker, J. (2018a). Digital technologies as external enablers of new venture creation in the IT hardware sector. *Entrepreneurship Theory and Practice, 42*(1), 47–69.

von Briel, F., Recker, J., & Davidsson, P. (2018b). Not all digital venture ideas are created equal: Implications for venture creation processes. *Journal of Strategic Information Systems, 27*(4), 278–295.

Waizenegger, L., McKenna, B., Cai, W., & Bendz, T. (2020). An affordance perspective of team collaboration and enforced working from home during COVID-19. *European Journal of Information Systems, 29*(4), 429–442. https://doi.org/10.1080/0960085X.2020.1800417.

Chapter 2
Information Systems in the COVID-19 Pandemic: An Analysis of Infection Dashboards and Their State-Tracking Abilities

Fritz Hädrich

Abstract Information systems play a great role in informing people, politicians, and CEOs about the current state of the COVID-19 pandemic and in improving their decision making. A popular way to do this is to use dashboards that visualize the current state of infections, deaths, and recoveries in a given area. In this chapter, three popular infection dashboards are empirically analyzed, compared, and evaluated in terms of their quality and ability to faithfully present information based on guidelines of representation theory. Besides, the state of the literature on representation theory and infection dashboards is presented. The findings show that the dashboards vary in their coherence and do not consider external events which leads to an unfaithful representation of changes during the pandemic. Three popular dashboards are ranked, and suggestions are given on how to improve them by fulfilling the external event condition of representation theory. This also helps to design future dashboards more faithfully.

Keywords Infection dashboard · Representation theory · Information systems · State-tracking model · Empirical COVID-19 data · Geographical COVID-19 infections · COVID-19 numbers

Introduction

The COVID-19 pandemic arising in early 2020 is a huge disruption to almost all businesses, private lives, and research around the globe. It is a major challenge for humanity and demands all areas to commit to decreasing its impact on people, businesses, and society as a whole. Therefore, scientists from various research fields try to fight the virus and its consequences. The information systems (IS) field cannot directly battle the virus but has the potential to help other fields do so, for example,

F. Hädrich (✉)
University of Cologne, Cologne, Germany

C. Hovestadt et al. (eds.), *Digital Responses to Covid-19*, SpringerBriefs in Information Systems, https://doi.org/10.1007/978-3-030-66611-8_2

by providing relevant and accurate information, as well as making information accessible. Information is key when it comes to decision making by politicians, businesses, and people. There is a vast amount of data regarding healthy, infected, recovered, or deceased people all over the globe. Getting useful information out of that data and presenting the right information at the right time are key challenges for information systems. Digital artifacts like web dashboards promise to display relevant information through clear and intuitive diagrams and other visualizations. Representing numbers of infections, recoveries, and deaths should be seen as critical since doing it carries risks of misinformation and fraud. If the visualizations are ambiguous or miss out on critical developments, they can misinform the decision making of their users which in turn can harm a lot of people. This becomes clear by looking at the monthly users of such dashboards: For example, the homepage of the German federal health research institute, the *Robert-Koch-Institut* (RKI), had over 66 million visits in March 2020 (SimilarWeb 2020) and these users are offered a dashboard which also received millions of views. Imagine displaying biased or even false information to this amount of people, including politicians who may be influenced in their decision making with human lives at stake. The RKI dashboard is even embedded in the official website of Thüringen (a German state) which emphasizes the closeness between politicians and such dashboards (Corona. Thueringen 2020). In Germany, there is a saying that translates to "do not trust any statistic that you did not fake yourself", and even if these representations in the dashboards are not manipulated on purpose they still should fulfill design specifications defined by representation theory to be reliable. If the quality of a dashboard is high and the specifications of representation theory are applied sufficiently, the dashboard can serve as a useful and efficient source of information. In this essay, we look at the cases of three popular infection tracking dashboards and analyze them regarding their quality and ability to track changes in the real world and represent them faithfully.

High quality infection tracking dashboards that can faithfully track and display changes of the pandemic are useful to fight it. But are the commonly used dashboards designed that way? Do they offer valuable information or are they susceptible to misinformation? The goal of this analysis is to evaluate how good of an information system these dashboards are and how reliably they represent the changes of the COVID-19 pandemic. By analyzing them with regard to their state-tracking abilities and their quality, the currently used dashboards can be improved, and the development of future dashboards can be supported. Improved dashboards would offer better ways to fight pandemics now and in the future since COVID-19 will likely not be the last ever pandemic. Furthermore, the research field of representation theory is extended by this analysis.

The remainder of the chapter unfolds as follows. In the next section, the state of the literature regarding representation theory and COVID-19 dashboards is presented. This is followed by a description of the research method. Then, the "Findings" section presents the results of the analysis, which involves describing, evaluating, and comparing the different dashboards to each other. After a brief discussion of this work's limitations, a conclusion is given, including a grading of each dashboard. The final section covers an outlook for future research and practice.

State of the Literature

Displaying data regarding the COVID-19 pandemic in a dashboard can be classified as a representation of real-world data through an IS, which in turn is investigated by the field of representation theory. An especially relevant aspect of representation theory is *state-tracking*, which refers to maintaining a representation (or *tracing*) of phenomena as they change (Recker 2020). The databases *Google Scholar* and *IEEE Xplore* have been searched for literature regarding representation theory in IS. The most relevant papers on state-tracking are summarized and discussed by Recker et al. (2019), who provide a review of theory and evidence of representations in IS. They summarize relevant aspects of representation theory that are used in the analysis of this essay to examine the usefulness of the dashboards. First, the *representation model* ensures that the scripts generated by IS grammars are faithful representations of real-world phenomena (Wand and Weber 1995). Second, the *state-tracking model* comprises four requirements that information systems need to adhere to in order to faithfully track dynamic real-world phenomena. Third, the *good-decomposition model* provides conditions for the script to communicate more meaning about real-world phenomena (Wand and Weber 1995).

All three models increase the quality and usefulness of an IS. However, for dashboards that represent the COVID-19 pandemic, the state-tracking model is especially important since the pandemic is seen as an ever-changing process to be modeled and this can only be done by faithfully tracking changes of states (Recker 2020).

In addition to the existing literature on representation theory, literature about the dashboards that represent the pandemic has been searched. As early as 6 months after the start of the pandemic there are already several publications dealing with this topic: Some researchers have developed data visualizations or own dashboards (e.g., Hamzah et al. (2020), Posch et al. (2020), Florez and Singh (2020)). Other research focuses on the future development of the numbers of infected people, such as Javid et al. (2020) and Kriston (2020). A comprehensive review by Latif et al. (2020) summarizes the findings of papers produced during the pandemic and papers including not-yet-peer-reviewed papers. This review analyzes datasets and repositories that dashboards are built upon and highlights challenges and pitfalls. When it comes to papers that have similar research goals like this one, the results of IEEE Xplore and Google Scholar showed zero publications.

Method

To make the research process of this essay transparent and to ensure reproducibility, the applied methodology is described briefly in this section. Knowing about the methodology will also help the reader to better understand the results. To get access to the newest publications dealing with representation theory and dashboards representing COVID-19 data, several keywords have been searched for in different databases. The databases searched are mainly Google Scholar and IEEE Xplore. The search strings were composed of the keywords ("representation theory" AND "dashboards"), "COVID-19 dashboards", "COVID-19 pandemic dashboards", "analysis of COVID-19 dashboards" and some additional synonyms of these terms. Since the COVID-19 pandemic is a unique and disruptive event, only publications from 2020 onwards have been searched if "COVID-19" was included in the search terms. Besides, only publications in English and German have been considered. The search was conducted in June and July 2020. By doing this, the state of the current literature in this field is presented. After determining the state of the literature, dashboards for deeper analysis have been selected. The selection was based on popularity but also on diversity. For example, after choosing to analyze the RKI Dashboard, the dashboard of the Johns Hopkins University was excluded from the choice set due to their similarity (both of them are designed by ESRI, a software company specialized in geographic IS). To allow for each dashboard to be analyzed in sufficient depth, the choice of dashboards was limited to three. One of them is only covering data for Germany, one is specialized in Germany but also offers data for the whole world, while the third is designed for the world. The analysis consists of three parts: First, each part of the dashboard is described from top to bottom. Second, each part is reviewed regarding user-friendliness, readability, and coherence (summarized as quality). Third, each part of the dashboard is checked against the four conditions of the state-tracking model. This is followed by a discussion about the drawbacks of this methodology and the difficulties that arose. Afterwards, the main results are summarized, and the dashboards are graded and compared. Finally, an outlook on future research and practice is given.

Findings

In this section, the dashboards of the RKI, the *Berliner Morgenpost*, and the *World Health Organization* (WHO) are described, analyzed, and evaluated with regards to their quality and state-tracking abilities. They are described systematically from top to bottom to ensure every dashboard component is considered.

RKI Dashboard

The RKI dashboard is published by Germany's main federal health research institute. According to SimilarWeb.com, the RKI dashboard's visits seem to correlate with the number of COVID-19 infections in Germany. The monthly visits increased from January 2020 with 1.7 million to March 2020 with 66.6 million, and decreased to 21.7 million in May 2020 and 16.8 million in June 2020, which is still a very high number compared to the German population of 83 million (SimilarWeb 2020). Therefore, the dashboard has a wide reach and a high impact on informing or misinforming the German population. A screenshot of the dashboard's default view is shown in Fig. 2.1. The dashboard is available at https://corona.rki.de.

The website of the RKI dashboard consists of several panels that display different data based on selections by the user. The size of each panel can be adjusted individually to help to focus on the information the user is interested in. The top-panel includes the headline "Robert Koch-Institut: COVID-19-Dashboard" and has an option to select whether the information should be presented on the granularity of states (broader) or of districts (finer). If the user selects one of these options, the presented information in the other panel changes. For each other panel, there is an option to enlarge it by clicking on the top right corner of it. These functionalities of increasing the size of a panel are helping the user to focus but do not provide benefits for panels that don't show more information after increasing their size (for example the bottom left corner panel that only shows the date of the last data update).

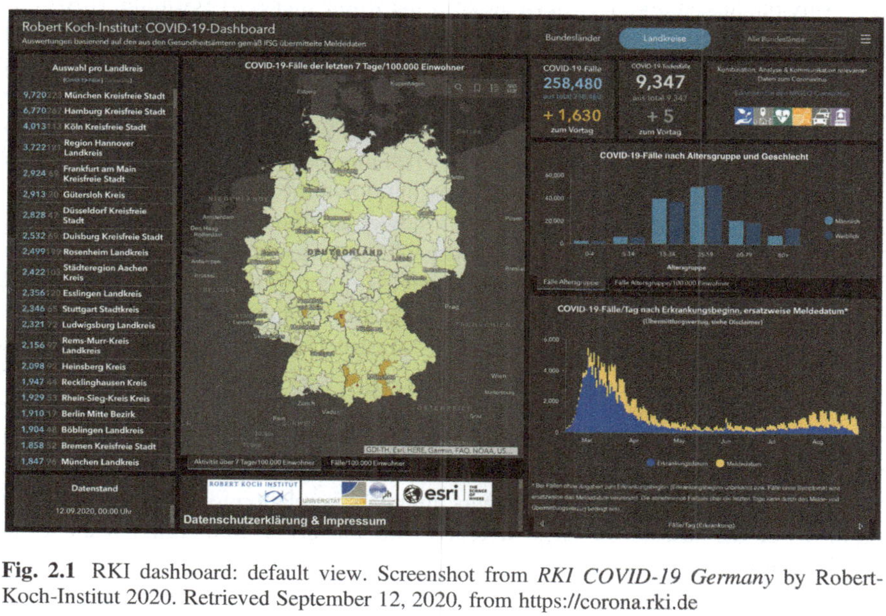

Fig. 2.1 RKI dashboard: default view. Screenshot from *RKI COVID-19 Germany* by Robert-Koch-Institut 2020. Retrieved September 12, 2020, from https://corona.rki.de

Fig. 2.2 RKI dashboard: expanded map panel with one district selected. Screenshot from *RKI COVID-19 Germany* by Robert-Koch-Institut 2020. Retrieved September 12, 2020, from https://corona.rki.de

The central panel (shown expanded in Fig. 2.2) consists of a map that focuses on Germany but has an option to navigate over the whole planet by scrolling. However, there is no data for countries other than Germany. This design choice can be assessed as bad for several reasons: One reason is that the focus of the whole dashboard is Germany, thus there is no real need to include other countries. Another one is that the implementation of the worldwide map comes along with loads of geographical data (no data about the pandemic) to be loaded when the dashboard is opened and kept in the computer's memory, consequently slowing down the whole website and bringing performance problems to users with slower internet connections. Moreover, implementing a map of the whole world without presenting data for the whole world can be seen as ontological incompleteness or a construct deficit as described by Wand and Weber (1993). This might lead to users employing other grammars to compensate for the missing ontological constructs (Wand and Weber 1993, pp. 227–228). Translated to dashboards, this could lead to users switching to other dashboards to compensate for the missing data on the rest of the world. Besides, the user can click on the states or districts on the map to receive information about that region presented in another little panel that pops up on the top left of the map-panel, as shown in Fig. 2.2. Here, total numbers, numbers in relation to the population, and numbers of the last seven days in relation to the population (only available at districts) are displayed. In addition, the number of inhabitants is shown, followed by the total number of deaths. The latter is neither shown in relation to the total population nor for the last seven days. Therefore, it is difficult for the user to examine the real-world state by looking at almost raw data. Nevertheless, the districts are colored based on their case numbers of the last seven days which delivers insights into which district is currently especially affected by the pandemic compared to others. Here, the information is put into context and illustrated with colors that help the user retrieving useful information out of the dashboard. When states are selected, they are only colored by their total numbers in relation to their population instead, which is less informative and inconsistent. This visualization fulfills the mapping condition from representation theory, which states that every state of the real-world phenomena must map to at least one state in the IS (Recker et al. 2019, p. 769). In COVID-19-dashboards, this means that it should be feasible for users to determine relevant status indicators for particular collectives of people which is possible here (Recker 2020). Additionally, the tracking condition is fulfilled, which states that if internal events change the state of things, the IS must faithfully represent both, the first state and the subsequent state (Recker et al. 2019, p. 770). For dashboards, this necessitates being able to track changes for relevant collectives of people (Recker 2020). In a small toolbar in the top right of the map-panel, there are options to change the map. The user can search for a specific district to be zoomed in on the map, select a state to be zoomed in from a dropdown menu, inform themself about the different colors used, or change the type of the map (e.g., satellite, topographic, or streets). For a user who is just interested in the actual state of the situation, this can be assessed as information overload with 12 styles of maps to choose from. On the other hand, for further analysis of whether some characteristics of different areas might have correlations with the COVID-19 case numbers, these different map styles might be of use.

Nevertheless, for a more precise representation of the real-world, an option to display external impacts and events would be more helpful than steady topologies of the map. Since this is not implemented, the external event condition is not satisfied, which states that if an external event occurs in the real-world, an external event that is a faithful representation of it must occur in the IS (Recker et al. 2019, p. 770). Besides, on the bottom left of the map-panel, the user can choose between total case numbers or case numbers for the last 7 days, both in relation to the population if districts are selected (for states, the total case numbers are available). This makes the switch between total cases and latest cases fairly simple, which is helpful since the map panel is offering a lot of information, especially in the district mode.

The panel on the left (Fig. 2.1) offers a list of Germany's districts (or states, depending on the selected mode) ranked by their case numbers and additionally showing the numbers of COVID-19-related deaths. This panel serves a crucial function as clicking on a state or district changes all data input for the other panels on the dashboard.

The panels on the top right present information about the total numbers of infections and deaths for the selected region as well as the changes of these numbers compared to the previous day and compare these numbers to the total numbers for Germany as a whole. Only in state-mode, the number of recovered people is also shown, which has a "~" symbol in front of them indicating that this number is an estimate, which is further explained in a disclaimer. If recoveries are considered essential information to be represented by the dashboard (i.e., they are a relevant change of a state), this would be a violation of fulfilling the tracking condition of representation theory. A person that recovers from an infection should be represented faithfully since it is a thing that changes its state.

Below that, there is a panel that displays the cases of the selection grouped by age and gender either in total or in relation to the population as a bar chart. The gender is displayed in the same different shades of blue as used in the map panel, but the colors have a different meaning in this panel. This can be either assessed as coherent since the user is familiar with these shades of blue or it can be assessed as irritating since the same color now delivers different information. Despite the design, the differentiation of gender and age delivers more detailed information to the user and is necessary for faithful state-tracking.

On the central bottom side of the dashboard, there is a panel containing the dashboard's privacy policy and imprint, but this is of no further significance to the analysis in this essay. The panel on the bottom left shows the date of the last data update and also offers the option for full-size, which is just hiding the other panels and offers no additional information. Additionally, the user can click on the date to highlight it in blue which again serves no further utility. These options that have no useful purpose can be assessed as unnecessary options that lower the user-friendliness.

The panel on the bottom right contains a second bar graph for the selected region that displays the number of infections per day since the start of the pandemic. It is shown in its expanded form in Fig. 2.3. The colors blue and yellow separate the infections that have started on the given day and infections for which this day is not known and are therefore assigned to the day on which they have been reported to the

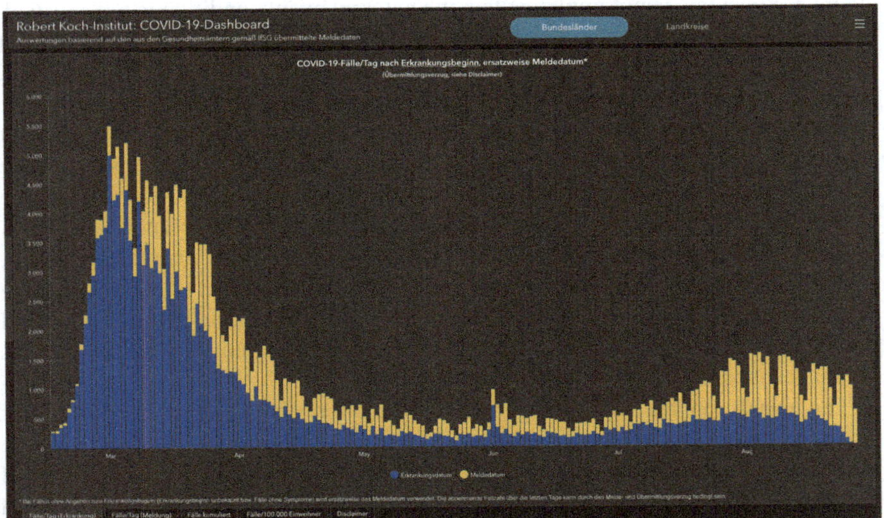

Fig. 2.3 RKI dashboard: expanded daily infection number panel. Screenshot from *RKI COVID-19 Germany* by Robert-Koch-Institut 2020. Retrieved September 12, 2020, from https://corona.rki.de

authorities. This panel clearly shows when the pandemic reached its peak in the selected region and consequently presents the famous curve that the whole world is trying to flatten (vox.com 2020). This bar graph is highly informative since the user can select any state or district of Germany and analyze the course of the pandemic from early March until today. The progress over time of the bar graph serves as an indicator for the future development of COVID-19-cases and can be used for analysis that can help to reduce or prevent infections, not only for the selected region.

Sadly, external measures and changes that directly influence those numbers are being considered neither by the bar graph in this panel nor the whole dashboard. If a user tries to identify correlations between external events and their impact on COVID-19-cases, additional information is needed to come to valid conclusions. Representation theory describes this as not fulfilling the external event condition. Further, at the bottom of this panel, the user can select how the COVID-19 cases should be presented in the graph of this panel. Selectable options are infections (per day, by date of infection), reported cases (per day, by the day the infection was reported to the RKI), or the cumulative number of reported cases. These are all displayed by a vertical bar chart that shows the famous curve for the selected region. The fourth option is the number of infections in relation to the population for each federal state (or district, not per day), which is represented as a horizontal bar chart. For the first three options, it is very important that the displayed order of new infections matches the order of infections in the real world. Changes displayed in the dashboard must be ordered in the same way they occurred in the real world and are not allowed to be cached and put into the system later and at random (Wand and Weber 1995, p. 213). Even though Wand and Weber (1995) refer to the correct order of external events that are not considered by the dashboard (Recker 2020), the statement can also be applied to the sequence of reported cases. Additionally, the tracking condition of representation theory is violated if the dates of infections are incorrect or in wrong order because if the date of the displayed infection is false, the state change is not represented faithfully.

Nevertheless, the disclaimer that there might be a delay in transmitting data from the local health agencies to the RKI is used to provide as much information as needed to understand when the state of the thing (i.e., a person is infected) changed. The separation of "beginning date of illness" (blue) and "reporting date" (yellow) points out that the user has to be careful with the interpretation of these dates. The dashboard not only marks these possible inaccuracies but also mentions in a statement on the bottom of this panel that "a decreasing number of cases over the last days can be explained by a delay in reporting and transmission of data". Consequently, possible misinterpretations are prevented which can be assessed as a positive aspect of the dashboard, although state-tracking conditions might be violated. Moreover, the infections in relation to the population shown by the fourth option in this panel are not specific to the selected state or district but are represented by a bar chart that displays the 10 districts which are affected the most by the pandemic or all 16 states ranked by their cases. This is a bad design choice since a user would most likely expect the whole panel to be about the selected state or district because all other selections in this panel do refer to a specific state or district.

The bottom of the bottom-right panel and a separate panel on the left of the website (opens by clicking on a triangle button) contain the same disclaimer with important information about the data presented. Here, the terms used in the graphics are explained and the accuracy of the data is clarified. It is stated that the exact date of individual infections cannot be determined. Moreover, it is stated that the RKI in fact uses verification algorithms to validate the data received from the local health agencies. But due to the high dynamics of the situation, some data is published before undergoing quality checks or validation. The transparency of the quality of the data used is evaluated positively but the quality of the data presented is unsatisfactory low. This evaluation is congruent with Skiera et al. (2020), who suggest further complementation of these numbers by Google search and Twitter data.

In general, the colors chosen to represent the graphics are not that intuitive since a lot of different shades of blue and orange are used instead of signal colors like red and green. If the data for some district or state is not accessible, this is shown by little warning triangles. By doing this, possible misinterpretations can be prevented. For users who are interested in the number of worldwide cases, the disclaimer points to the WHO, whose dashboard is analyzed as the third dashboard in this section.

Berliner Morgenpost Coronavirus Monitor

This dashboard is published by the German newspaper *Berliner Morgenpost*. It has been selected for analysis for its popularity as the monthly visits increased from January with only 140,000 to April 2020 with an outstanding 50.8 million and, as the pandemic slowed down, decreased to 30.6 million in May 2020 and to 18.4 million in June 2020, which is still a very high number (SimilarWeb 2020b). The number of visits is lower than those of the RKI dashboard until April 2020 and higher thereafter. Due to copyright reasons, we are unable to show screenshots of the dashboard in this book, so please have a look at it yourself at https://interaktiv.morgenpost.de/corona-virus-karte-infektionen-deutschland-weltweit (Berliner Morgenpost 2020).[1]

This dashboard displays a map of the world that can additionally be zoomed in on Germany or Europe by using the buttons in the upper left. The unique design element of this dashboard is the representation of COVID-19 case numbers using three-layered circles located in the middle of their corresponding country or state. The circles consist of three different inner circles colored red for infected people, green for recovered people, and black for deceased people. Using circles instead of

[1]You can also use the Internet Archive at https://web.archive.org in case the dashboard is no longer available at the time you are reading this book. This link points directly to a version of the dashboard as it looked at the time of writing: https://web.archive.org/web/20200914230720/; https://interaktiv.morgenpost.de/corona-virus-karte-infektionen-deutschland-weltweit/.

coloring the whole country has the benefit that it is possible to display information about three different things at the same time compared to only one. This makes it easier to track changes, consequently fulfilling the tracking condition. Each circle's size depends on the number of infected/recovered/deceased people in total and is put in relation to the population of the country or state. By hovering over any circle, a small popup is displayed which shows the actual numbers represented in the three circles, as well as the same numbers per 100,000 inhabitants, and the date of the last update.

This is an elegant way to display basic information about a country or state as the user does not have to click anything, and the colors chosen are easy to distinguish and intuitive to understand. However, it neither offers information about past COVID-19 statistics of the region nor does it foreshadow anything likely to happen in the future. By zooming into the map of one country, the cases get grouped by states instead of one circle for a whole country (this feature is available for selected countries only, including Germany). This feature supports the mapping condition since by zooming in, relevant states for relevant collectives of people are displayed.

Besides the map, on the left part of the dashboard, the numbers of total cases (either from Germany, Europe, or worldwide) are presented. The numbers are matching the colors from the circles which is a congruent design choice. When selecting "Europe" or "worldwide", it is noticed in a footnote that the number of recovered people is not originating from official government sources. In all three selection modes including "Germany", the approximately equal sign ($\approx$) is placed before the number of recovered people, which is misleading (it gets clarified at the bottom of the website) because all German states report numbers of recovered people in contrast to other countries (e.g., Great Britain does not report any number for recovered people). This can be seen as a violation of the mapping requirement of representation theory since relevant information is missing for particular collectives of people. It definitely is a violation of the tracking condition of representation theory as it is not possible to track relevant changes in states for relevant collectives of people. Arguably, recoveries are not the most relevant information displayed by the dashboards, but they are still one of the major information displayed and should fulfill state-tracking conditions. Especially since it is one of the only two possible state changes after being infected, it becomes more and more relevant over the course of the pandemic to be able to put the cumulative number of infections into context. Above these numbers, the date of the last data update is displayed, highlighted in yellow, and below the numbers the user can how the numbers changed since the last day (again separated by infected/recovered/deceased with the same colors as in the circles).

Further, users have the option to change the whole dashboard from displaying total numbers to displaying new infections of the last seven days by clicking on a small switch (or directly clicking at "new infections"). This is a useful feature that helps users to inform themselves about the current course of the pandemic concerning its timely and geospatial shift.

Depending on the selection, below that the user either sees a line chart with all cases aggregated since the beginning of the pandemic (again structured by infected/

recovered/deceased) or looks at a bar chart of new cases that have been reported in the last two weeks. The displaying of two weeks in the diagram allows the user to compare the current week to the last one. An arrow serves as an indicator for the development of the numbers of new infections: A red arrow indicates increasing infection numbers compared to the last seven days and a green arrow displays decreasing numbers. The arrows get steeper if the change of numbers is bigger. This feature is important because it describes how the pandemic process unfolds over time. It is similar to the bottom right panel of the RKI dashboard and even shows the famous curve if total cases are selected. The curve presented here is containing more information than just aggregated cases: Additionally, the recoveries and the deaths are visible in the diagram which makes it possible to instantly subtract recovered people from the total number of infected people. This additional information improves the quality of the curve diagram and facilitates a better tracking of state changes which satisfies the tracking condition.

Below the graphs (either the curve graph or the new infections graph), the numbers corresponding to the selected graph are displayed in a table per German state (or per country, if the "Europe" or "worldwide" tabs are selected). There are two tabs, one where the table shows the absolute numbers and one where it shows the relative numbers per 100,000 inhabitants. In the new infections mode, there is an option to click on "last 7 days" or "daily average". This is considered useless since clicking either of these two does not change anything related to the information displayed because data for both options is displayed all the time. It only changes the style of the clicked text to be bold. It is to mention that the table also contains cruise ships, although they are not part of the ranking but are just the bottom entry. If cases per 100,000 inhabitants are selected, there is no data input for cruise ships, and on the map, there is no circle visible for them. It can be argued about the usefulness of implementing data of cruise ships but in general, information that is accurate and fulfills conditions of the state-tracking model is always a good addition. The described tables provide a ranking of countries and states with regard to their cases, deaths, and recoveries meeting mapping and tracking conditions but not the external event condition.

At the bottom of the map, there is a sliding bar that can be used to select any date since the start of the pandemic. This is a time traveling option that changes the whole dashboard to show only the data up to the selected day. This feature offers a lot of information that can be analyzed and can hopefully ultimately help in fighting the pandemic. By moving the slider slowly from earlier dates to later ones, the course of the pandemic in affected regions is illustrated. Although timely and geospatial shifts help to understand the development of the pandemic, there are no representations of external events included that influence or explain these shifts. The dashboard only offers an illustration of the course without considering external events like lockdowns, rules and legislations, or specific behaviors of a collective of people in its representations. This violation of the external event condition of representation theory leads to a decline in the usefulness of the dashboard since important information influencing the pandemic is not faithfully tracked. Displaying the course without displaying the events that shape the course ultimately lowers the quality of the dashboard, for example by not offering visualizations of correlations and possible causations. Furthermore, next to the sliding bar there is a button that serves the same function as the aforementioned small slider in the left section of the dashboard, that is, it switches between the total infections mode and the new infections mode. Consequently, the changing of almost all data that is represented in the dashboard can be done in multiple ways that are all distributed between the graphics. Since this function has a major effect on showing the current development of the process of the pandemic instead of displaying just aggregated numbers (even though the lack of external events has to be considered when interpreting it), it would be better if this functionality was implemented on a central area on top of the website instead of several (redundant) buttons or switches.

Other than the main dashboard described up to this point, the Berliner Morgenpost dashboard also offers a newsfeed on the lower part of the webpage and two additional graphics that focus on a smaller map (e.g., local areas within states). The first of the two maps displays Germany with its districts that are colored on a scale between green and red if there is currently a high risk of a regional lockdown.[2] This map represents new infections in the last seven days in relation to the population of every district, delivering relevant information to users that live in these areas. The classification of the main dashboard into countries and states has the potential to disguise critical local areas. For example, the impact of the superspreading at *Tönnies Holding GmbH & Co. KG* with over 1000 infected employees in June is (almost) not visible in the main dashboard but becomes clear in the more detailed map (Tagesschau.de 2020). Again, external events like the mentioned superspreading at Tönnies are not considered by the dashboard, but at least their impacts are visible in the detailed map. The fact that this visualization is not supplemented with external events declines the usefulness of the dashboard because it no longer faithfully represents the real-world phenomena (Recker 2020).

The second graphic focuses on an individual district of Germany selected by the user and breaks the previously described circles down into the municipalities within it. By offering these visualizations, more detailed information about regions that are of higher relevance to the respective user is represented. Finally, one last visualization at the bottom of the website represents the basic reproduction number R_0 for Germany which is defined by Dietz (1993) as "the number of secondary cases which one case would produce in a completely susceptible population", that is, a population with no preexisting immunity. If it is above 1 (i.e., 1 infected person infects on average more than 1 person) the graph is colored red, otherwise, it is green. This is an efficient representation of the state of the current situation of Germany, but again without fulfilling the external event condition.

On the bottom of the website, there is some information regarding the data sources, which are for international data inter alia the WHO and for national data the RKI. In addition, some clarifications are given with regard to different methods

[2]There is a political agreement in Germany that a local lockdown must be implemented in a district if infection numbers exceed 50 per 100,000 inhabitants.

of data supply which can lead to unrealistic numbers. These explanations are necessary to not provide false information or mark information that does not display the real-world but looks like it does. For example, the negative 30,000 cases in the United Kingdom on 3 July 2020 are explained (change of reporting method by the United Kingdom). The approximately equal sign in front of numbers for German recoveries is explained, too. Without this explanation, this would be misleading, but with the explanation, it is clear that the numbers for recoveries are partly estimated due to the non-existing notification requirement. Summarizing, the additional information about data sources and the dashboard in general is very comprehensive and helps to understand what is being displayed.

WHO Coronavirus Disease (COVID-19) Dashboard

The *World Health Organization* (WHO) is a global agency responsible for public health. It was founded in 1948 as an agency of the United Nations (World Health Organization 2020a). Since the COVID-19 pandemic endangers the health of people worldwide, it is of interest to take a deeper look at the dashboard provided by the WHO. The dashboard is accessible at https://covid19.who.int/. A screenshot of the dashboard's default view is shown in Fig. 2.4.

When it comes to visits to the dashboard, it cannot compete with the numbers for example by the RKI dashboard analyzed before, it also falls behind the Berliner Morgenpost dashboard. Its visits in April 2020 were about three million and rose to almost four million in May 2020, and slightly decreased to 3.6 million in June 2020 (SimilarWeb 2020c).

The dashboard offers a big search bar on top of a worldwide map where it is possible to search for a country, territory, or area. Next to the search bar, there is an information button that leads to a page offering relevant information about the data the dashboard is presenting, as well as an option to download the data. Next to the information button, there is a sharing button that brings up a popup providing options to share the link to the dashboard via social media or email. On the top right, there is a donation button to donate directly to the WHO's *COVID-19 Solidarity Response Fund.* This is a good extension as it provides an additional way to fight the pandemic (helping directly by donating) that is not available on the other presented dashboards.

On the left of the map, the user can choose between a choropleth map (default, shown in Fig. 2.4) and a bubble map (shown in Fig. 2.5). Below that, the user can select "cases" or "deaths", and the map will change accordingly. For the former, the map uses shades of blue, for the latter it uses shades of orange. In a dropdown menu further below, the user can determine whether they want to see absolute numbers, numbers in relation to the total population, the percentage change in the last seven days, the absolute newly reported numbers for the last seven days, or the absolute newly reported numbers for the last 24 h. The final option, transmission classification", is only available for case numbers on the choropleth map. If this is selected,

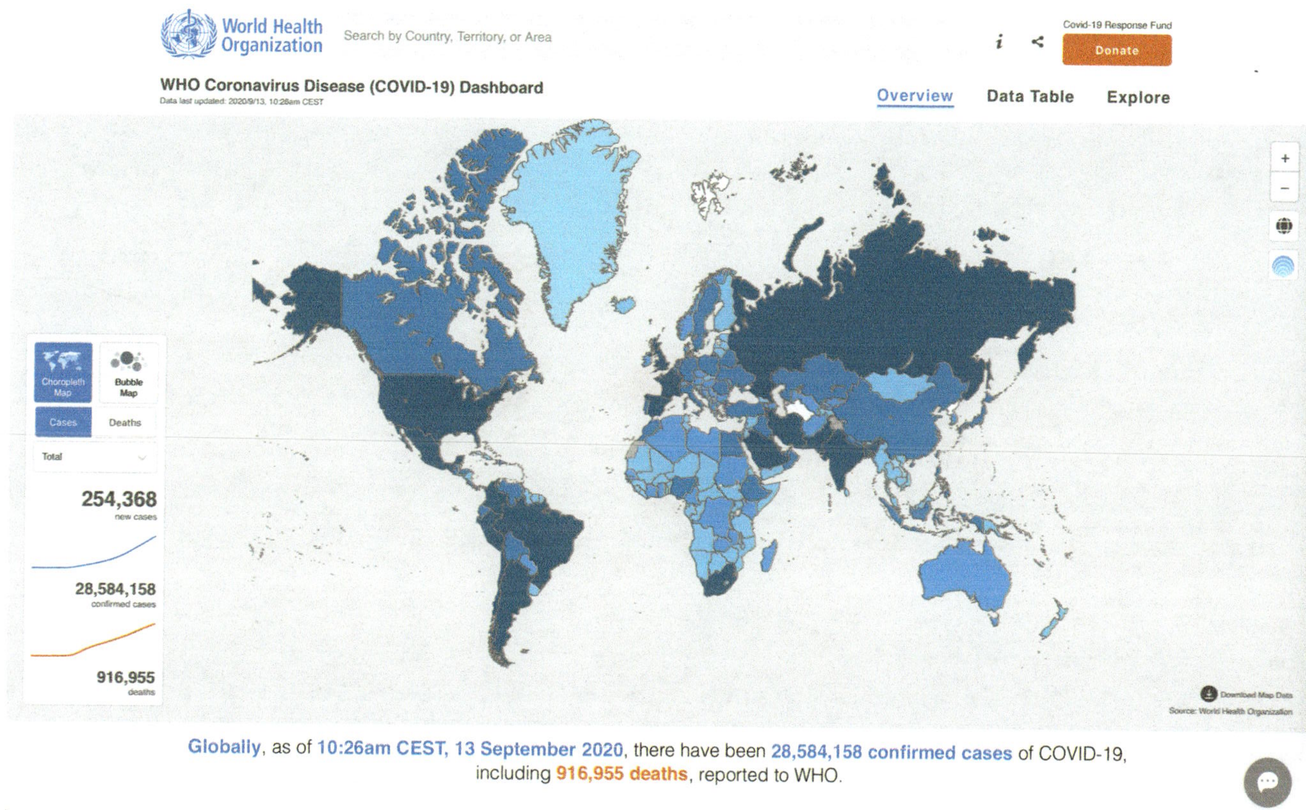

Fig. 2.4 WHO dashboard: default view (choropleth map). Screenshot from *WHO Coronavirus Disease (COVID-19) Dashboard* by World Health Organization 2020b. Retrieved September 12, 2020, from https://covid19.who.int

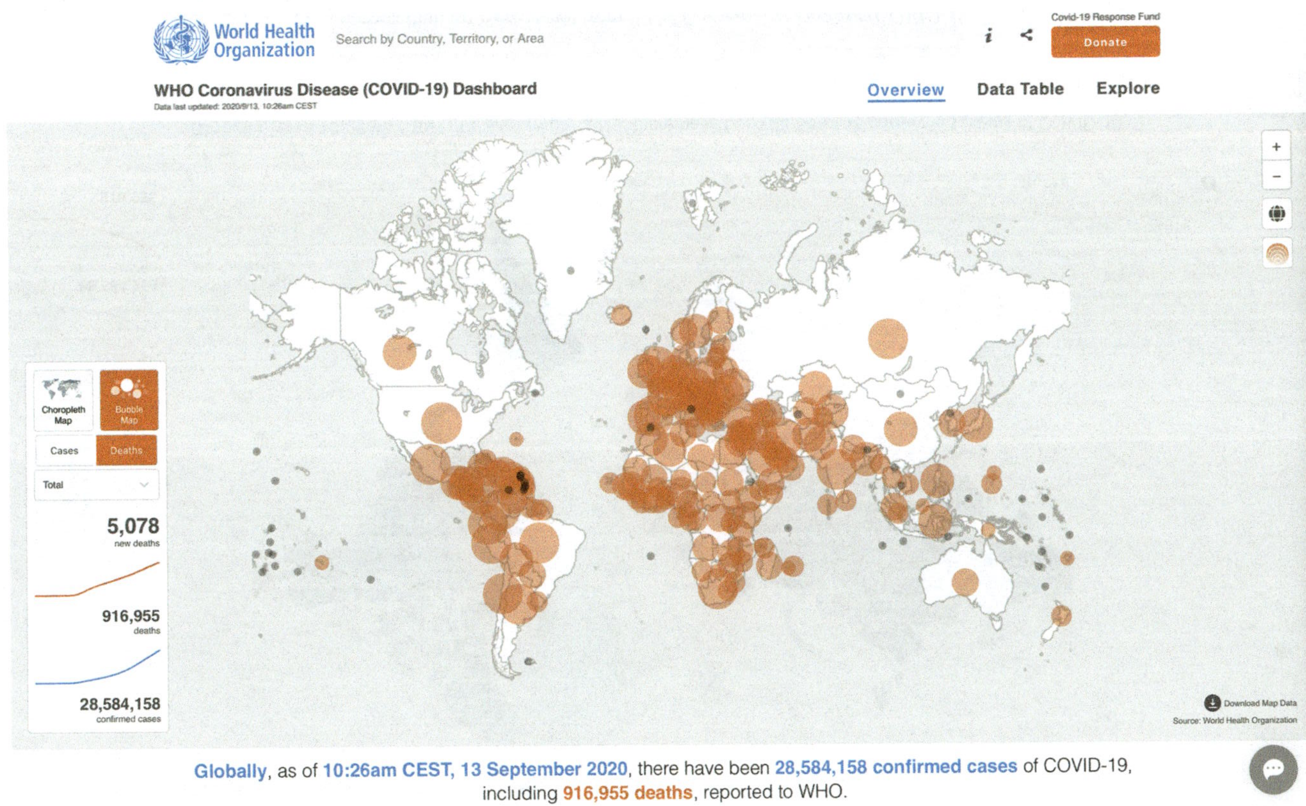

Fig. 2.5 WHO dashboard: main view with bubble map. Screenshot from *WHO Coronavirus Disease (COVID-19) Dashboard* by World Health Organization 2020b. Retrieved September 12, 2020, from https://covid19.who.int

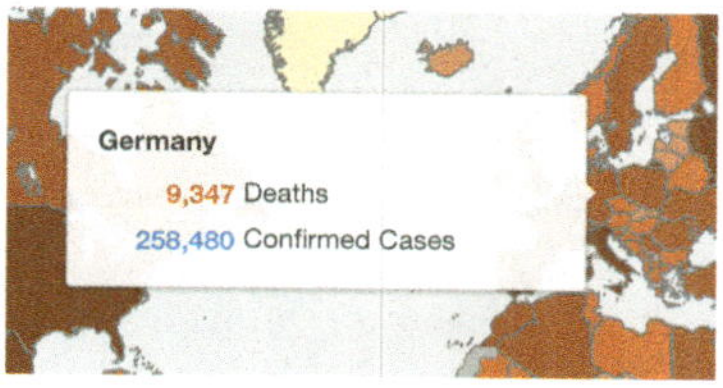

Fig. 2.6 WHO dashboard: popup shown when hovering over a country. Screenshot from *WHO Coronavirus Disease (COVID-19) Dashboard* by World Health Organization 2020b. Retrieved September 12, 2020, from https://covid19.who.int

each country is colored based on its case numbers and how these cases are distributed within the country. The transmission scenarios distinguish between no cases, sporadic cases, clusters of cases, and community transmission. This visualization provides a general overview of how the cases emerged within each country but is not detailed enough to fulfill the conditions of the state-tracking model.

The actual numbers are shown in a popup when hovering over the countries (Fig. 2.6). Recoveries are not shown at all, which is a violation of the tracking condition of faithful state-tracking. In contrast to the other two dashboards, the number of people that recovered from the virus is not even estimated or mentioned in any graphic. When it comes to the mapping condition, it is not fulfilled as satisfying as in the other analyzed dashboards as the dashboard offers no option to distinguish between different groups of people nor different municipalities within a country. Not even for countries large in size and population such as the USA the user can distinguish between states. Therefore, the information presented is not very precise and can be regarded as being of comparatively low quality.

On the left of the map, below the described options of what to present, two line graphs are shown that are designed in a minimalistic style as they have neither axes nor labeling. They are surrounded by three numbers, and it is not immediately clear which number belongs to which graph. The three numbers are labeled "new cases", "confirmed cases", and "deaths".[3] Since one of the graphs is blue and the other is orange, it is likely that the graphs relate to the numbers below them, that is, the blue one represents "confirmed cases" and the orange one "deaths", while there is no graph for "new cases". This visualization is unclear and not properly explained. Consequently, no tracking condition is fulfilled by this part of the dashboard.

On the bottom of the map, a sentence briefly summarizes information about the country selected, namely the number of cases and deaths and the date of the last data update. If no country is selected, the global numbers are displayed instead.

Below this sentence, there are two bar graphs (Fig. 2.7), one displaying confirmed cases and one displaying deaths of the selected country (or global if nothing is selected). These graphs are right beneath each other so that the days are in the same position on their x-axis on both graphs. This design facilitates the direct comparison

[3] If "deaths" are selected, the labels change to "new deaths", "deaths", and "confirmed cases".

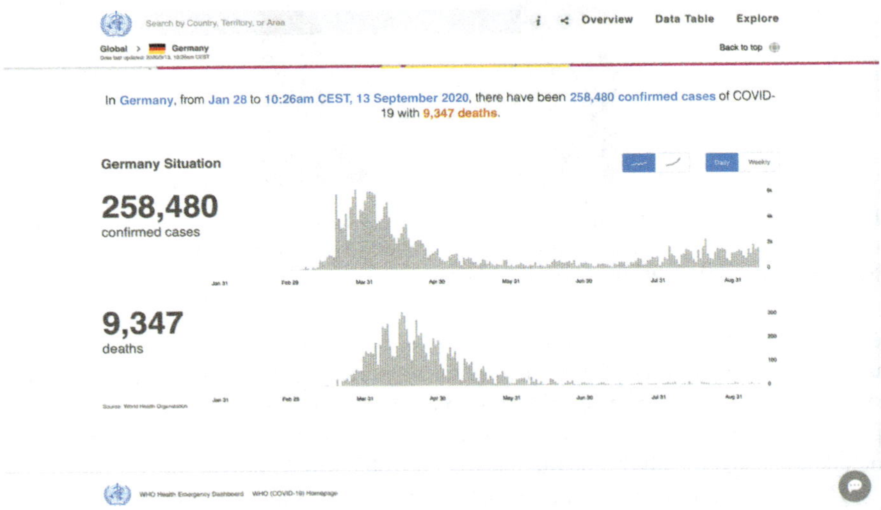

Fig. 2.7 WHO dashboard: bar charts below the main map. Screenshot from *WHO Coronavirus Disease (COVID-19) Dashboard* by World Health Organization 2020b. Retrieved September 12, 2020, from https://covid19.who.int

of confirmed cases and deaths for specific days for the whole pandemic. In the top right there are two switches: One for switching between "daily changes" or "cumulative curves" and another for switching between daily or weekly bars. The latter option does lower the amount of information presented but it averages out differences between working days and weekends. By hovering over them, the numbers for confirmed cases, daily (weekly) increase, as well as daily (weekly) change in percent are shown. In summary, these graphs facilitate tracking of changes over time but do neither consider anything causing or influencing these changes, nor do they offer details like regional shifts, demographics of people infected/deceased, or population density of the region. These graphs are similar to the curve graphs of the other two dashboards (and met the same state-tracking conditions) but have the advantage of more effectively presenting when exactly the deaths occurred compared to numbers of cases. The Berliner Morgenpost dashboard also offers this feature, but the scaling of the y-axis is not adjusted which makes it harder to clearly see the correlation. The RKI dashboard has no death numbers visible in its curve graph.

If no country is selected, the two bar graphs represent global numbers. In addition, there are colorful representations of data for the WHO regions (can be compared to continents) beneath them (Fig. 2.8). In the top right the same options as for the bar graphs are present, but there is a further option to select "per 1 million population", that displays relevant information with regard to the population size.

All regions are displayed in one bar graph with different colors. On the left, there is a ranking of the regions including their numbers (either cases or deaths). If

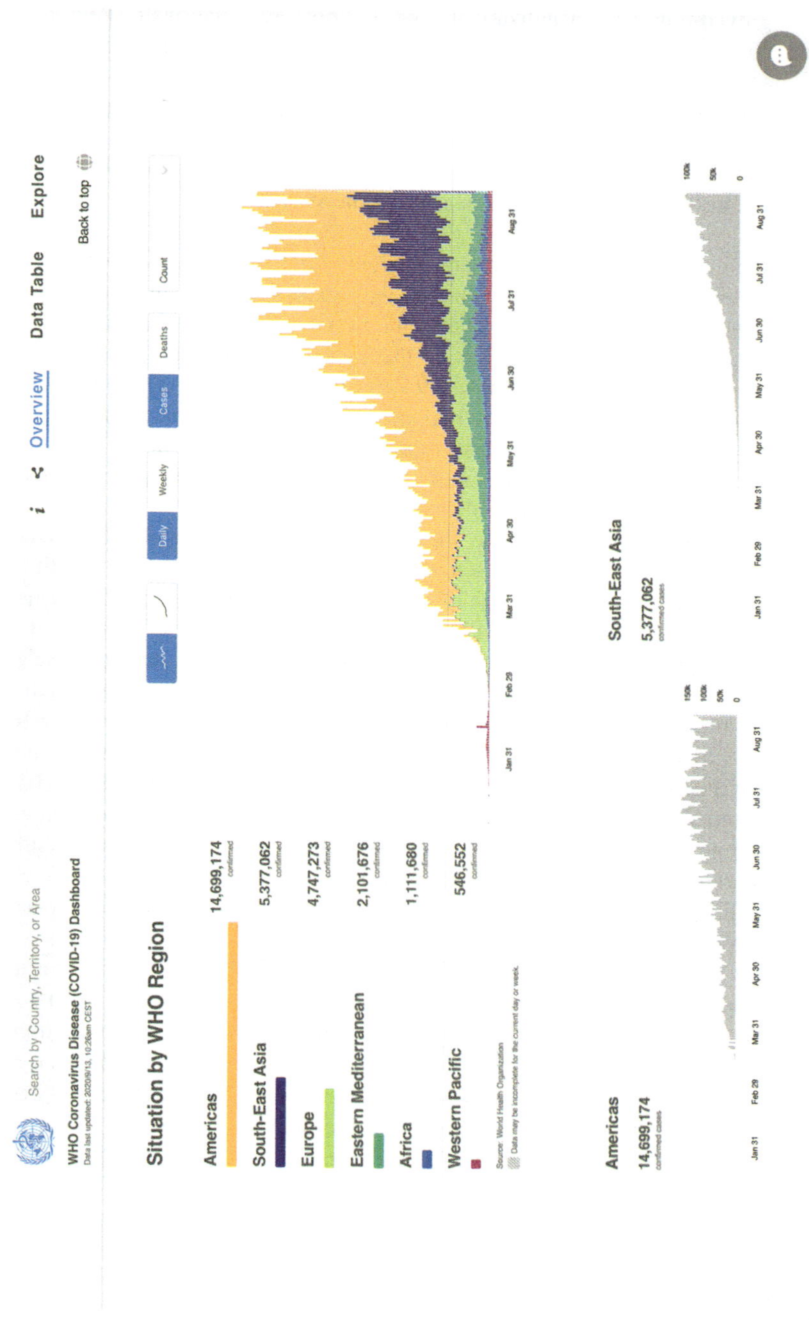

Fig. 2.8 WHO dashboard: bar charts below the main map. Screenshot from *WHO Coronavirus Disease (COVID-19) Dashboard* by World Health Organization 2020b. Retrieved September 12, 2020, from https://covid19.who.int

hovering over a region, its corresponding part in the bar graph is colored and the others are greyed out. This visualization offers to compare situations by region but still lacks faithful state-tracking abilities by neither considering external events nor relevant changes in states (e.g., recoveries). Below the graph that combines all regions, a separate graph for each region is presented that adds the information of daily (weekly) change and daily (weekly) increase. Nevertheless, the individual graphs do not bring more to the table when it comes to faithfully track states since the daily (weekly) change could also be seen in the visualizations of the combined graph.

At the bottom of the website, there are diagrams for 12 countries shown that are not changeable (Fig. 2.9). It is not explained why these countries are chosen to be visualized. The visualizations are similar to the previous ones despite that they are line charts instead of bar charts. One of the presented countries is the United Kingdom, whose daily cases are minus 29,726 on July 3, 2020. This impossible number of confirmed cases might have happened due to a correction of numbers by the local authorities (correcting for over-reportings in the days before), but this is neither marked as such nor is it explained to the user. The displayed graphics are wrong when it comes to representing the real world.

Finally, on top of the whole website, there is a button labeled "Explore" to switch to a different website that provides one scatter plot diagram with three axes, with the third axis being represented by the size of circles (Fig. 2.10). For each axis, the user can choose between "confirmed cases", "cumulative cases", "deaths", "cumulative deaths", and "population". A fourth drop-down menu offers the option to select countries that are highlighted in the plot. This scatterplot delivers more information than the other presented graphs described earlier and additionally offers a sliding bar right beneath it to select any date of the pandemic period. This feature, which is also to be found in the Berliner Morgenpost dashboard, offers a lot of information to help to fight the pandemic, especially due to its three different customizable axes that can be used. Despite the positive aspects of such an illustration, there are still neither external events considered nor is the data accurate at the WHO dashboard. By moving the slider back and forth, dots emerge that are placed left from the y-axis and below the x-axis which makes no sense. For example, the Netherlands and Norway have negative "confirmed cases" on March 23, 2020. This shows that the WHO dashboard uses the raw data and supplies its visualizations without validating individual data points and without further explanation to prevent misinterpretations.

There are two further positive aspects of the dashboard: First, on the bottom right corner, there is a chatbot offered to answer questions the user types in or selects from a Frequently-Asked-Questions section. Second, the displayed data for the current week is always marked to symbol the incompleteness of it.

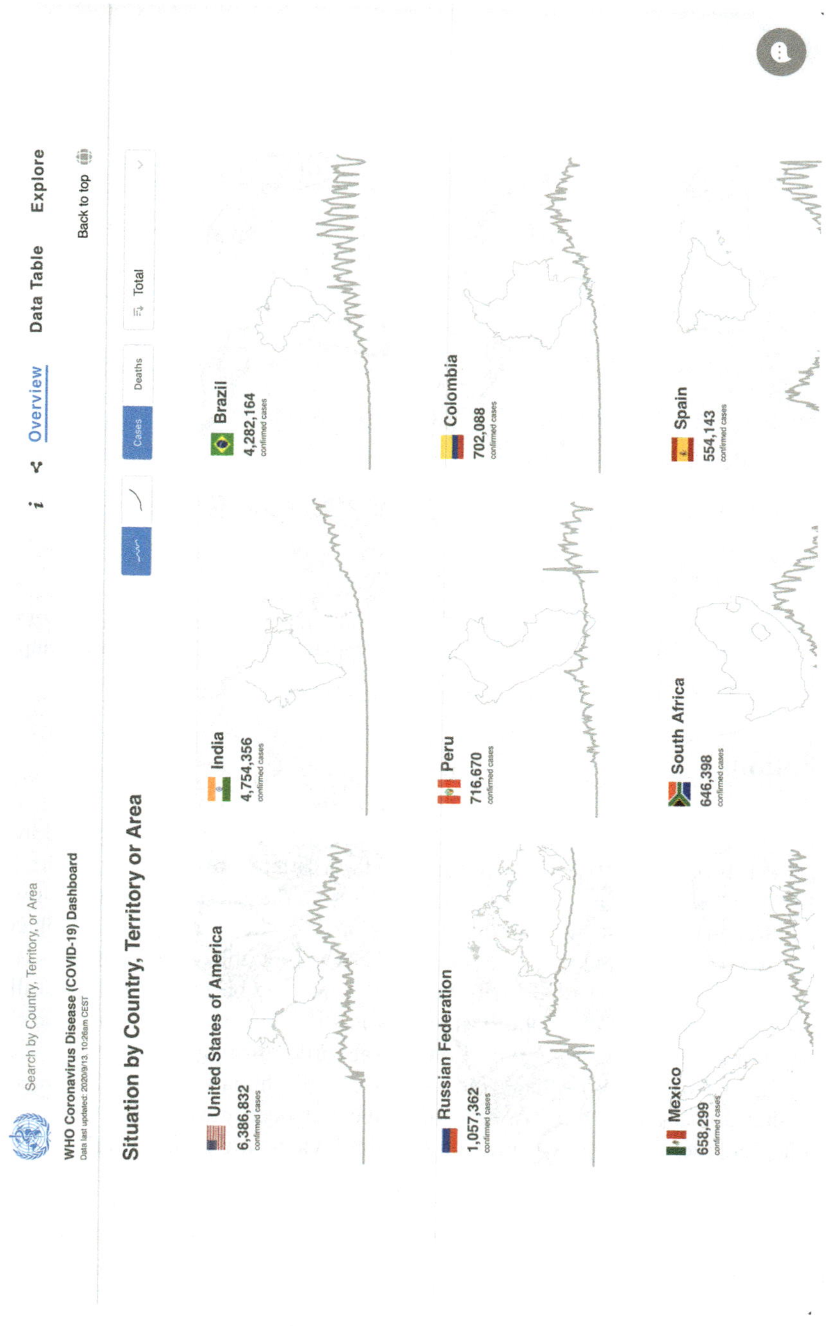

Fig. 2.9 WHO dashboard: bar charts for situation by country. Screenshot from *WHO Coronavirus Disease (COVID-19) Dashboard* by World Health Organization 2020b. Retrieved September 12, 2020, from https://covid19.who.int

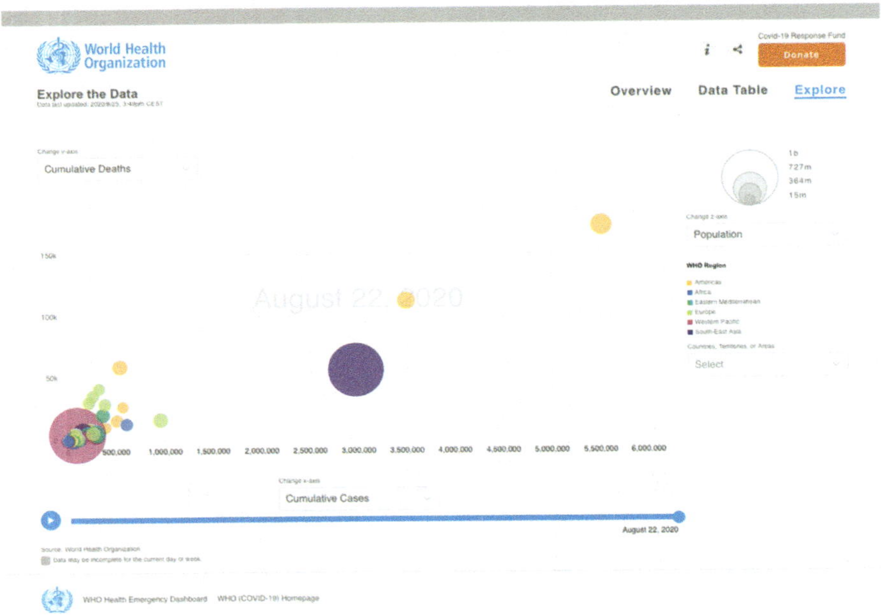

Fig. 2.10 WHO dashboard: explorer tab. Screenshot from *WHO Coronavirus Disease (COVID-19) Dashboard* by World Health Organization 2020b. Retrieved August 22, 2020, from https://covid19.who.int

Limitations

First, when analyzing how many visits the dashboards had, it was difficult to address the dashboards individually and not count visits to a parent website. For example, the numbers for "rki.de" are very high but for "corona.rki.de" they are way lower (around three million visits per month). Additionally, for the specific URL displayed in the browser, the utilized resource *SimilarWeb* was not able to present any data. Therefore, the numbers of total visits per month need to be interpreted carefully. Nevertheless, the relevance of the dashboards is still high even if the numbers of visits are not as enormous as 66.6 million but one order of magnitude lower.

Second, to completely evaluate the quality of a dashboard, further analysis is needed that considers various aspects that have not been covered by this essay. Examples include the responsiveness on mobile devices, the general performance, the design of the backend, and the quality of the data used. This essay solely focuses on the general coherence and the fulfillment of the state-tracking model.

Third, the volume of infection testing differs significantly by country, which leads to high variations in the accuracy of the number of infected people. This is a big problem when aiming at representations that truly display the state of the real whole world since the dashboard can only display data that has been collected. For example, US President Donald Trump actively reduced the number of tests to manipulate data before it can be displayed faithfully (CNN.com 2020). Limitations like this have to be considered when extracting information out of the dashboards.

Finally, it has to be considered that the analyzed dashboards are under continuous development and some of the described functionalities may change in the future.

Conclusion

In conclusion, the Berliner Morgenpost Coronavirus Monitor offers the most helpful representations of the three analyzed dashboards. Its design is easier to interpret for the user due to its intuitive colors. Furthermore, the circles are a clever design choice to display the numbers of cases, deaths, and recoveries at the same time. Furthermore, the visualizations and data sources are explained in detail to prevent misinterpretations of the displayed information. In contrast to this, the WHO dashboard lacks clarifications that would put its visualizations in context. It is also less detailed when it comes to meeting the mapping condition and offers no data about recoveries. Its "Explorer" is a powerful and unique tool to represent a lot of data, but it comes along with reduced user-friendliness and also does not fulfill the external event condition. Finally, the RKI Dashboard is ranked in between the other two. It offers detailed information concerning geographical and demographic collectives but lacks intuitive design and user-friendliness. Also, it is the only dashboard of the three that considers the age and gender of infected people.

Table 2.1 compares the results of the analysis regarding the dashboards' quality and the four state-tracking conditions from the state-tracking model of representation theory. An "A" symbolizes good quality or respectively the fulfillment of the respective condition. "B" stands for medium quality and only partly fulfilling the condition. Finally, "C" represents bad quality and not at all fulfilling the condition.

Since external events are not covered on any part of the three dashboards, they are all graded as C. Consequently, they all also do not satisfy the sequencing condition of the state-tracking model because this condition refers to the sequence of external events that are not considered (Recker et al. 2019, p. 770). When choosing a dashboard to get information, the Berliner Morgenpost Coronavirus Monitor should be recommended due to its coherence and satisfaction of at least the mapping and (for the most part) the tracking condition. Nevertheless, the analyzed dashboards

Table 2.1 Comparison of dashboards

Dashboard	Quality/ coherence	Mapping condition	Tracking condition	External event condition	Sequencing condition
RKI	B	A	B	C	C
Berliner Morgenpost	A	A	B	C	C
WHO	C	B	B	C	C

need to be improved by considering external events and meeting the external event and sequencing conditions to stay faithful at representing the real world as the pandemic continues.

Outlook

Based on the state of the current research regarding dashboards that display the data about the COVID-19 pandemic, there is a lack of guidelines and analysis of how to faithfully do this. Future research should focus on clear guidelines that have to be fulfilled by a dashboard to inform the public about the true state of the real world. More research needs to be conducted to improve existing dashboards since the literature review resulted in zero publications dealing with this at the time of writing. The analysis showed that the three analyzed dashboards are not considering external events and have sometimes failed to display correct data about the real-world. For practice, this means to improve the existing dashboards and extend them by displaying external events that shape the pandemic's course. Including measures, activities, and events in the visualizations has the potential to show important correlations and causations that can help to understand and fight the pandemic.

References

Berliner Morgenpost. (2020). *Berliner Morgenpost Coronavirus-Monitor*. Retrieved September 12, 2020, from https://interaktiv.morgenpost.de/corona-virus-karte-infektionen-deutschland-weltweit/

CNN.com. (2020). *Trump now says he wasn't kidding when he told officials to slow down coronavirus testing, contradicting staff*. Retrieved July 12, 2020, from https://edition.cnn.com/2020/06/22/politics/donald-trump-testing-slow-down-response/index.html

Corona.Thueringen. (2020). *Coronavirus-Informationsportal der Landesregierung*. Retrieved July 12, 2020, from https://corona.thueringen.de/

Dietz, K. (1993). The estimation of the basic reproduction number for infectious diseases. *Statistical Methods in Medical Research, 2*(1), 23–41. https://doi.org/10.1177/096228029300200103.

Florez, H., & Singh, S. (2020). Online dashboard and data analysis approach for assessing COVID-19 case and death data. *F1000Research, 9*, 570. https://doi.org/10.12688/f1000research.24164.1.

Hamzah, F. B., Lau, C., Nazri, H., Ligot, D. V., Lee, G., & Tan, C. L. (2020). CoronaTracker: Worldwide COVID-19 outbreak data analysis and prediction. *Bull World Health Organ, 1*, 32.

Javid, A. M., Liang, X., Venkitaraman, A., & Chatterjee, S. (2020). Predictive analysis of COVID-19 time-series Data from Johns Hopkins University. ArXiv Preprint ArXiv:2005.05060

Kriston, L. (2020). *Aktuelle Entwicklung der kumulativen Inzidenz bestätigter SARS-CoV-2-Infektionen und infektionsbedingter Todesfälle in Deutschland* [Modeling the cumulative incidence of SARS-CoV-2 cases and deaths in Germany].

Latif, S., Usman, M., Manzoor, S., Iqbal, W., Qadir, J., Tyson, G., Castro, I., Razi, A., Boulos, M. N. K., & Weller, A. (2020). Leveraging data science to combat COVID-19: A comprehensive review

Posch, M., Bauer, P., Posch, A., & König, F. (2020). Analysis of Austrian COVID-19 deaths by age and sex. *Wiener Klinische Wochenschrift., 132*, 685–689. https://doi.org/10.1007/s00508-020-01707-9.

Recker, J. (2020). *Aiding the management of crisis situations through effective state-tracking: Lessons learnt from research on IS as representations*. Unpublished working paper, version May 2020.

Recker, J., Indulska, M., University of Queensland, University of Cologne, Green, P., Queensland University of Technology, Burton-Jones, A., University of Queensland, Weber, R., & Monash University/University of Queensland. (2019). Information systems as representations: A review of the theory and evidence. *Journal of the Association for Information Systems*, 735–786. https://doi.org/10.17705/1jais.00550.

Robert-Koch-Institut. (2020). *RKI COVID-19 Germany*. Retrieved September 12, 2020, from https://corona.rki.de

SimilarWeb. (2020). *Traffic overview*, June 2020. Retrieved July 7, 2020, from https://www.similarweb.com/website/rki.de#overview

SimilarWeb. (2020b). *Traffic overview*, June 2020. Retrieved July 7, 2020, from https://www.similarweb.com/website/interaktiv.morgenpost.de/#overview

SimilarWeb. (2020c). *Traffic overview*, June 2020. Retrieved July 7, 2020, from https://www.similarweb.com/website/covid19.who.int/#overview

Skiera, B., Jürgensmeier, L., Stowe, K., & Gurevych, I. (2020). How to best predict the daily number of new infections of COVID-19. ArXiv Preprint ArXiv:2004.03937

Tagesschau.de. (2020). *Corona-Ausbruch bei TönniesViele Infizierte*, null Vertrauen, June 2020. Retrieved July 14, 2020, from https://www.tagesschau.de/inland/toennies-coronainfektionen-guetersloh-101.html

Vox.com. (2020). *The US doesn't just need to flatten the curve. It needs to "raise the line"*, April 2020. Retrieved July 14, 2020, from https://www.vox.com/2020/4/7/21201260/coronavirus-usa-chart-mask-shortage-ventilators-flatten-the-curve

Wand, Y., & Weber, R. (1993). On the ontological expressiveness of information systems analysis and design grammars. *Journal of Information Systems, 3*(4), 217–237.

Wand, Y., & Weber, R. (1995). On the deep structure of information systems. *Information Systems Journal, 5*(3), 203–223.

World Health Organization. (2020a). *Who we are*. Retrieved July 4, 2020, from https://www.who.int/about/who-we-are

World Health Organization. (2020b). *WHO Coronavirus Disease (COVID-19) Dashboard*. Retrieved from https://covid19.who.int

Chapter 3
Case Study: The Corona Contact Tracing App in Germany

Lorenz Kriehn

Abstract The long lasting COVID-19 pandemic is a burden on daily life and a serious health threat. One tool to control the pandemic's spread is *contact tracing*. Contact tracing means identifying and notifying all previously contacted persons of an infected person. This helps interrupting infection chains. This case study explores the challenges the developers, architects, and politicians faced during the development of the German *Corona-Warn-App*, a digital contact tracing application utilizing Bluetooth Low Energy (BLE). Possible privacy implications are analyzed based on the study by the creators of the contact tracing protocol *DP-3T*. Furthermore, digital contact tracing solutions of other countries are explored. European countries which have not released an app can benefit from the lessons learnt. Especially the involvement of the open-source community turns out to be beneficial.

Keywords COVID-19 tracing application · Bluetooth contact tracing · DP-3T · PEPP-PT · Privacy risk assessment · Corona-Warn-App

Introduction

The COVID-19 pandemic with over 240,000 cases and 9000 deaths in Germany until August 2020, has proven to be a long-lasting issue (Robert-Koch-Institut 2020a). After months of social distancing and worldwide shutdowns a potential vaccine is still months away. *Social distancing*—a collection of measures with the aim to keep people physically apart in order to reduce the spread of the virus—has proven to be a crucial part in managing the pandemic (Greenstone and Nigam 2020). The other main mechanisms to combat infections are isolating infected people, high hygiene standards, face masks, and contact tracing (Ferretti et al. 2020). The goal of

L. Kriehn (✉)
University of Cologne, Cologne, Germany
e-mail: lkriehn@smail.uni-koeln.de

C. Hovestadt et al. (eds.), *Digital Responses to Covid-19*, SpringerBriefs in Information Systems, https://doi.org/10.1007/978-3-030-66611-8_3

these mechanisms is to stop infection chains between infected people. This should contribute to reducing the number of cases and eventually eradicating the virus.

In Germany, workers of the local public health departments are currently tasked with tracing the contacts of all newly infected people and instructing them to self-quarantine and get tested. This involves three risks: First, it is a time-intensive activity and the number of health department workers is limited. Second, there is the risk of incomplete information as people need to remember everyone they have physically encountered in the last two weeks and they may not even know the names or the contact information of all those people. Third, the longer the process between the initial positive test result and the notification of all contact persons takes, the higher is the risk that an infected contact person has in turn infected other people before they are instructed to self-quarantine.

With the number of daily added cases decreasing, the restrictions that forbid close contact and meetings with more than two households are slowly being lifted. This opens the possibility of a "second wave" of new COVID-19 cases, as seen in the USA. Globally, new infection numbers are rising again and braking records for total daily new infections.

Especially in the current (August 2020) reopening phase in Germany, close contact with unknown people becomes more common again. As more and more people are coming back from their home offices and use public transport more frequently, the total number of contacts increases. Keeping track of those unknown contacts is not feasible for reasons of privacy and the amount of operational work that is needed.

To manage the number of contacts and to increase the speed at which contact persons are notified, while keeping the private contact and location data protected, a digital solution has been proposed: A smartphone application can utilize the existing Bluetooth hardware to identify potential exposures, which are situations where the corona virus could potentially be transmitted from one person to another. The app anonymously keeps track of all exposures and then, if the original person gets infected, anonymously notifies those contacts of their potential infection.

In this paper, I examine the question, how the German government handled the challenges during the planning and development of the German governmental COVID-19 contact tracing application, named the *Corona-Warn-App*. Other countries that have not released an app can learn from their decisions. Especially, other European Union countries can benefit from the lessons learnt, since their apps have to conform to similar laws and regulations. The source code of the Corona-Warn-App can be freely used and adopted since it is publicly available licensed under the *Apache License 2.0*. This could help smaller countries with smaller budgets or less expertise in data privacy and large software projects.

I will proceed as follows: In the next section, I give an overview of the current literature on the usefulness of contact tracing apps, the proposed design architectures, and implementations of different countries other than Germany. Afterwards, I discuss the case of the development of the German corona contact tracing application. Finally, I discuss the results, the implications, and give an outlook on further research questions.

State of the Literature

The pandemic has been ongoing for several months, but this is still a short time compared to the usual reviewing cycles in research. Nevertheless, some research results relevant to the research question of this paper have already been published, which will be presented in this section.

Ferretti et al. (2020) model the transmission of the corona virus using a mathematical approach. Their model can calculate the probabilities for different types of transmissions. They found that the most probable type of transmission with 47% is *presymptomatic* transmission, where an infected person infects another person before the onset of the symptoms. This is followed by *symptomatic* transmission (38%), where the disease is spread while the person shows symptoms. 10% of transmissions fall into the category of *environmental transmissions*, where the virus spreads over contaminated surfaces. The least common type are *asymptomatic transmissions* (6%), where the infectious person never shows symptoms (Ferretti et al. 2020). The fact that presymptomatic transmissions are the most common transmission type highlights the need to identify exposed people before they develop symptoms. This contrasts the common influenza virus, which spreads mostly over symptomatic transmissions (Ip et al. 2017).

Virus transmissions have an exponential nature; therefore, it is crucial to limit the spread early (Bar-On et al. 2020). An important indicator for the success of limiting the spread is the *basic reproduction number* R_0, which is defined by Dietz (1993) as "the number of secondary cases which one case would produce in a completely susceptible population" (i.e., a population with no preexisting immunity). In Germany, R_0 had the highest value of 3.38 on March 10, 2020 (Robert-Koch-Institut 2020b). Afterwards, it dropped to under 1 on March 20, 2020, and apart from a spike in June it has remained below 1.5 (Robert-Koch-Institut 2020b).

Figure 3.1, adapted from Ferretti et al. (2020), shows the importance of tracing and notifying contacts of infected people as fast as possible and how it is done via Bluetooth. The authors also show that, if enough people use digital contact tracing (around 60%), this can be enough to reduce the basic reproduction number R_0 below 1 even if no other countermeasures are in place (Ferretti et al. 2020). Nevertheless, it is not necessary to solely rely on the app for the management of the pandemic. Thus, a smaller user base can help containing the virus and it is not necessary to reach an active user base of 60% of the total population to realize a positive effect.

Tang (2020) analyzes the early digital contact tracing solutions of various countries regarding their workflow and privacy mechanisms. The author highlights the importance of using appropriate solutions for each culture. Some solutions that worked in China and South Korea (i.e., complete lockdown, facial recognition to trace contacts) are hard to implement in western cultures or do not conform with the respective country's privacy laws.

The author lists three future research directions, which could also be seen as potential challenges for contact tracing apps (Tang 2020):

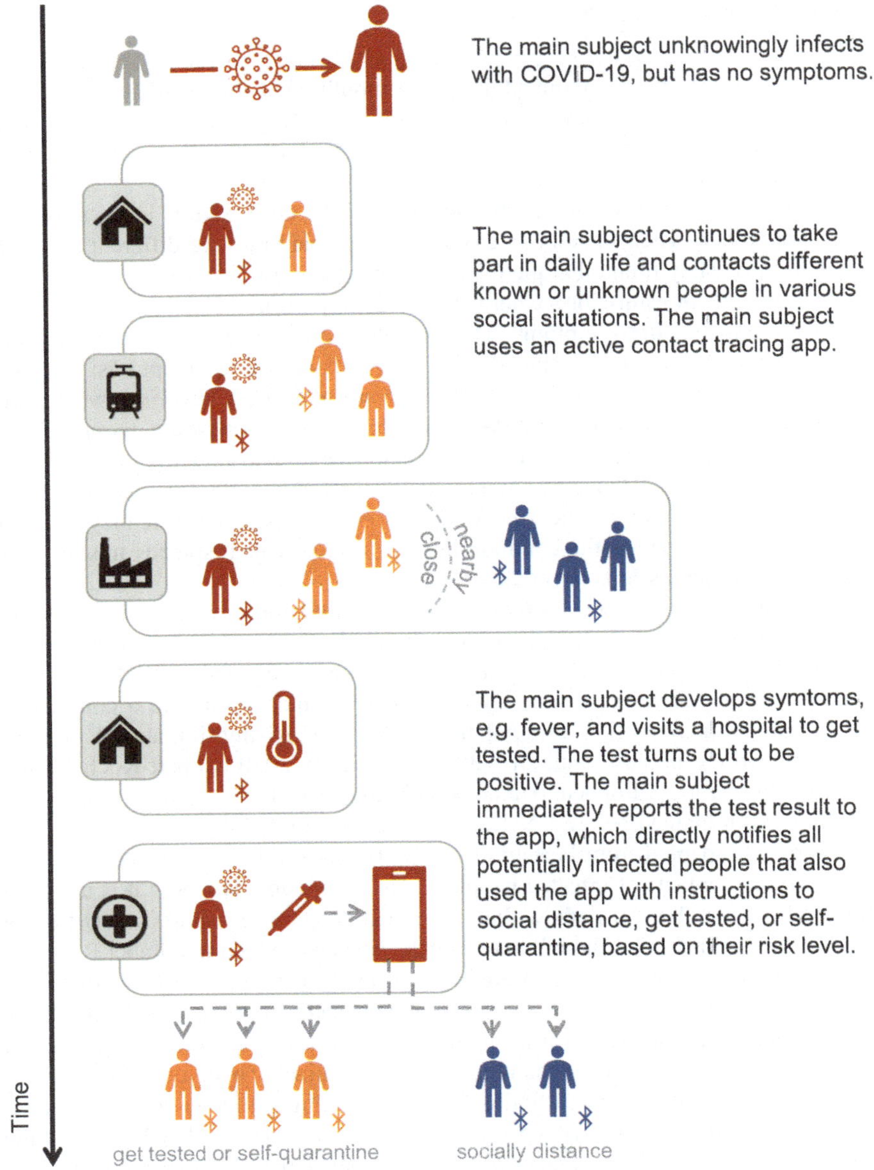

Fig. 3.1 An exemplary timeline of instant contact tracing. Adapted from "Quantifying SARS-CoV-2 transmission suggests epidemic control with digital contact tracing.", by L. Ferretti et al. 2020, *Science (New York, N.Y.)*, 368(6491), p. 619

1. Connecting the solution designers with the public health departments. This includes the development of medical-driven contact tracing.
2. Evaluating the privacy and security risks of given tracing solutions. That means clarifying the security requirements and explaining the tradeoffs between privacy, utility, and efficiency. Also, having clear accountability for the different parts of the app during the development and the production of the app.
3. Implementing incentives instead of a binary choice between "opt-in" and "opt-out". The solution should encourage honest behavior. The solution should implement technical restrictions to prevent surveillance use.

Tracing Model

To understand the privacy implications, it is important to understand the method contact tracing apps use to measure the contact between two smartphone users. I focus on the method using Bluetooth Low Energy (BLE). Another method could utilize the Global Positioning System (GPS), but using GPS alone is not viable because it is not precise enough indoors, where the risks of transmission is higher. GPS uses the absolute location, while BLE uses the relative location. Using the absolute location implies that the location data could be misused to create a movement profile for any user. This privacy risk combined with the inability to function during high risk encounters (indoors and in close proximity), means that GPS is not the preferred technology for contact tracing apps.

Apps using the BLE method try to measure the distance and contact time of an encounter between two people. Every smartphone where the app is active sends randomly generated tokens out in regular intervals, which other smartphones in physical range listen for and store as potential exposures. Additionally, the signal strength is measured and saved along the date of the contact. These identifiers are saved either decentralized on the receiving phone or on a central server, depending on the architecture.

Another important tool of those apps is the infection risk calculation. The app tries to calculate a number that represents the risk of an infection in case it detects an exposure to a person that is later tested positive. The app takes the signal strength measurement to approximate the distance between the two phones (and with that the distance between the two persons). Combining the distance measure and the total exposure time with an infected person, the infection risk level is calculated. If the calculated risk level is high enough, a warning is displayed. Additional information on how to act should be displayed and the person is asked to take a test.

Privacy Concerns

Tracing contacts between persons always bears risks of exposing private data and infringing privacy rights. This is less of a concern for the manual contact tracing done by the public health departments but a major concern for proximity tracing apps, since the public health departments only trace contacts after a confirmed infection based on the information the infected individual voluntarily shares. The fact that the data is collected and stored regardless of a potential infection allows for the possibility of a privacy breach. The danger comes from malicious intruders, an overreaching government, or the storing entity itself mishandling the data. There is also a concern that the implemented solutions might be kept longer then they need to be stored for the reason they were originally shared.

A first challenge is to decide which form of data collection is used. There are three distinct types: *Data grabbing* describes the collection of all available data with no respect to privacy concerns and use them to combat the pandemic. This is not legal in Europe due to the General Data Protection Regulation (GDPR). The second approach is an *anonymized data collection*. In this approach the data is stripped of identifying aspects, but true anonymization, in a sense that it is completely impossible to reconstruct who the data belongs to, is difficult to reach. This approach is already in use to combat the pandemic, for example, mobile data and telecom sensor data are already being analyzed to find out whether the initial lockdown measures (stay at home orders) were adhered to by the population (Offenborn and Kolvenbach 2020). The third approach are designs to *minimize the data collection*, which collect only specific kinds of data and do not rely on data collected by external or public infrastructures (Troncoso 2020).

Contact tracing apps are part of the third approach and can be categorized into two groups: *centralized* and *decentralized* approaches. In both approaches the app communicates with a central server, while the centralization property refers to where the data is stored: server-side (i.e., on central servers operated by the governmental authorities) in the centralized models and client-side (i.e., only on the individual user's phones) in the decentralized model.

The DP-3T team from the universities EPF Lausanne and the ETH Zurich analyzed the potential privacy risks of a proximity tracing system, the risks of a system that uses BLE, as well as the risks of the purposed methods to implement the proximity tracing via BLE. The main risks they found are:

1. The exposure notification can be used to identify persons that are infected. They state: "This risk is a consequence of the basic proximity tracing functionality and does not depend on any design choices or implementation details." (The DP-3T Project [DP-3T], 2020, p. 1). But, if there is any other contact tracing and exposure notification in place, for example, from the Health Departments, this risk is not increased by implementing the exposure notification in an app.

2. For all Bluetooth implementations:
   - The signal can be amplified with a powerful antenna and trigger false flag alarms. The mobile phone measures only the signal strength to calculate the difference and if the signal is artificially increased the distance measurement is wrong.
   - The Bluetooth signal can be disrupted through noise injection by a third party. This leads to failed contact discovery between two phones.
   - Users can be tracked through additional information provided by the phone. For example, MAC addresses are revealed if Bluetooth advertisements are not disabled. This depends on the firmware.
   - A user can identify locations with infected people by driving around and tracking the IDs coupled with the location of the Bluetooth handshake (so called 'wardriving').
3. The communication with the backend server could reveal identities to the provider and the server.
4. For decentralized systems where the infected person shares their identifiers, the backend server could track individual infected persons through those identifiers for the timeframe of the shared keys.
5. For decentralized systems where the infected persons share their collected identifiers, the backend server could learn about the social interaction of individual infected persons.

In the section "Privacy Risk Assessment" I analyze if and how these risks are present in the current implementation of the German *Corona-Warn-App*.

Early Solutions of Other Countries

To understand possible challenges for the German app, it is useful to look at the solutions of other countries for contact tracing apps.

Australia and Singapore both published a contact tracing app before Germany. Both of these work in a similar way, using BLE to confirm the proximity of the users. This data is saved on a central server. This choice of development comes with privacy concerns: The apps must be opened on the devices to work, since they do not use the (at the time unavailable) Application Programming Interfaces (APIs) developed by the major mobile operating system developers (Apple and Google) and have not implemented it since the release of the APIs. The fact, that the apps need to be opened at all times leads to high battery draining and incomplete tracing. People need to actively remember activating the app before meeting other people. This is a problem because the app is intended to track short and random encounters. Also, both people need to have it activated.

Norway suspended their app in early June 2020. They used GPS locations and BLE to track contacts. They also gathered the phone numbers, the age of the user, and other phone related data. The Norwegian public health institute concluded that "after having received a notification from the Norwegian Data Protection Authority imposing a ban on processing personal data collected by the app, the Norwegian Institute of Public Health (FHI) has temporarily suspended the use of the app, and will delete all personal data collected so far" (Norwegian Institute of Public Health [NIPH], 2020).

The contact tracing apps in Australia and China require the users to input personal information during the installation process. Because of the greater value placed on private data security and fear of getting tracked by the government, such a solution would be challenging to implement in Germany and could lead to resistance against the app in the population.

New Zealand used a simpler approach for their app: The app is seen as an addition to the work of the health department. It provides no contact tracing over BLE or other technologies. Instead, companies or organizations can apply for a QR-Code that visitors can scan with the app and record their visited places in a digital diary. In case of a positive test, the diary is then used by the health department to trace possible contacts (Ministry of Health – Manatū Hauora 2020). This solution is a digitalization of an analog process and includes no contact tracing. In Germany for example, the contact data of visitors must be gathered by law. It is unclear how this digital notebook helps containing the spread of COVID-19.

Other digital solutions are used with no regards to data privacy. For example, in Israel, the government authorized the intelligence service to use mobile data to trace the contacts of infected people. Normally this tool is only used against terrorists. The courts suspended the authorization because there was no monitoring of the intelligence service's actions by the parliament (Becker 2020).

The first main point to learn from the international landscape of contact tracing apps, is that a high level of privacy can be crucial to reach a wide audience in the population and not motivate a counter movement. The usage data of the Norwegian *Smittestopp* app suggests that nearly 60% of the users that downloaded the app never activated it or put the required personal data in. This shows the second main point, that an app needs a low entry barrier.

Case: German Contact Tracing App

In this section, I analyze how the German government managed the challenges during the development of the *Corona-Warn-App*. Figure 3.2 shows a timeline of significant events between the pandemic outbreak in Germany and the publication of the app.

In late March 2020, the German government commissioned and founded a German solution for a contact tracing application called "*Corona-Warn-App*". Two big national companies from the communication and technology sectors, namely *Deutsche Telekom AG* and *SAP SE*, were tasked with developing the

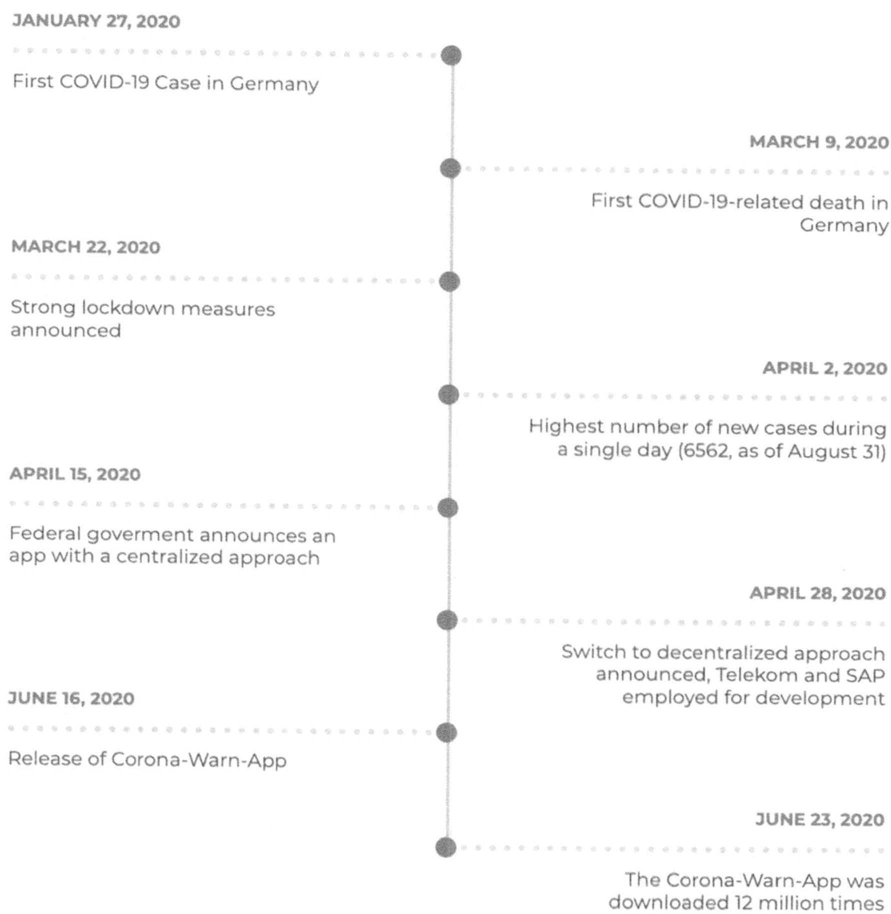

Fig. 3.2 Timeline of the Corona-Warn-App development in context of the COVID-19 pandemic in Germany

architecture and the application. The plan was to develop a mobile tracing application to help reopening the country and prevent further infection surges.

The main plan for the app was to provide a quick and anonymous way to trace contacts between people. In case of a positive test this information should be used to inform all contact persons of the exposure risks and lead to social distancing or quarantine of the exposed people. The notification should also provide access to a COVID-19 test, paid for by the health insurance. Especially at the start of the pandemic, the test capacity was insufficient to test every suspected case and only people with symptoms or with close contact to infected persons could be tested. Thus, a way to make informed decisions about who should get tested was a high priority.

The app is meant to complement the work of the health departments and is not intended to replace manual contact tracing. Instead, it should help tracing the exposed people who are unknown or forgotten.

Pan-European Approach

The first design approach was to follow the *Pan-European Privacy-Preserving Proximity Tracing* (PEPP-PT) protocol. PEPP-PT is not a single solution, but an open protocol designed to incorporate multiple solutions of European countries designed by European researchers. PEPP-PT's centralized approach led to many arguments about the usefulness versus the privacy impact of contact tracing apps. Offenborn and Kolvenbach (2020) quote the IT researcher and former professor Nadim Kobeissi, who said that the centralized approach assumes that the central instance is absolutely trustful and is trusted to never look at the saved data. He adds that this is a "crazy" assumption. They also quoted IT researcher Matthias Dalheimer who raised concerns of low acceptance and adoption of a tracking app in the population should a centralized approach be chosen.

In early April, major mobile operating system developers Google and Apple revealed their own contact tracing solution based on the DP-3T approach using BLE (Apple 2020). This implementation enabled a battery saving tracing solution which is always active in the background (in contrast to the Australian and Singaporean apps, which need to be activated manually). They use a decentralized approach to protect the user and to minimize the risk to expose private data. Still, Apple and Google's solution is only an API, which still requires a governmental app that builds on top of it and handles the identification of infected people. The apparent benefits of the Apple and Google API were enough to decide the German controversy about centralized or decentralized systems as the minister of health announced a switch to the decentralized approach (Turzer 2020).

Development

The initial idea of how to handle the source code was to make it open source after the development and deployment finished. After harsh criticism from privacy and IT experts, this decision was reversed and the whole development process was made public on the code hosting platform GitHub.

In the section "State of the Literature", I listed the challenges described by Tang (2020). The health authority and the solution designers were involved during the development of the Corona-Warn-App. Thomas Klingbeil of SAP SE explains the cooperation between the different partners (Dominik 2020): The software technology platform was provided by SAP SE, while the telecommunication provider Deutsche Telekom AG brought in the scalable infrastructure for the app. The research institutions Fraunhofer Institut and Helmholtz-Institut CISPA consulted the development team from SAP SE and Deutsche Telekom AG with insights into the Bluetooth technology and data privacy. The German federal governmental health research institute Robert-Koch-Institut (RKI) decided the parameter for the infection risk calculation.

This task allocation also contributes to solving the seconds challenge as there are clear accountabilities for each part of the app. Furthermore, security requirements have been formulated before starting the development.

The third challenge was not solved: There are no additional incentives for the user to use the app and there is only a binary choice to use the app or not. This is partly because one of the requirements of the app was that using the app should be completely voluntary and not using it should not lead to discrimination.

Rollout and Deployment

During the release press conference on June 16, 2020 (German Federal Government 2020), the open-source community work was regarded as a success for the project that helped build trust and resulted in a higher quality source code.

Although the goal of high adoption requires to create an app that had as few technological hurdles as possible, some older mobile phones were excluded. Mobile phones need to support BLE to run the app and since the app uses the Apple and Google API there are minimum operation system versions that are required. After the decision to use the Apple and Google API, the developers had no means to influence those requirements. This is a tradeoff the developers had to make. They chose a high functionality over a slightly higher number of total installations (roughly 10% of phones currently used in Germany do not fulfill the requirements). Figures 3.3, 3.4, 3.5, 3.6 and 3.7 show several screenshots from the app running on iOS.

The app reached 6 million downloads during the first few days, which increased to 14.6 million downloads after 2 weeks (Tagesschau.de 2020). Afterwards, the download numbers increased only slightly, reaching 17.5 million at the time of writing (August 31, 2020) (Frisse 2020). At the same time, the number of unique users that uploaded a positive test result was 2455, the first of which was uploaded on June 23 (Pfister 2020). The total number of positive test since the first user uploaded a test result at the same 52,441 (Robert-Koch-Institut 2020b). That means that during the first month nearly 4.7% of the total positive tests were recorded by the app.

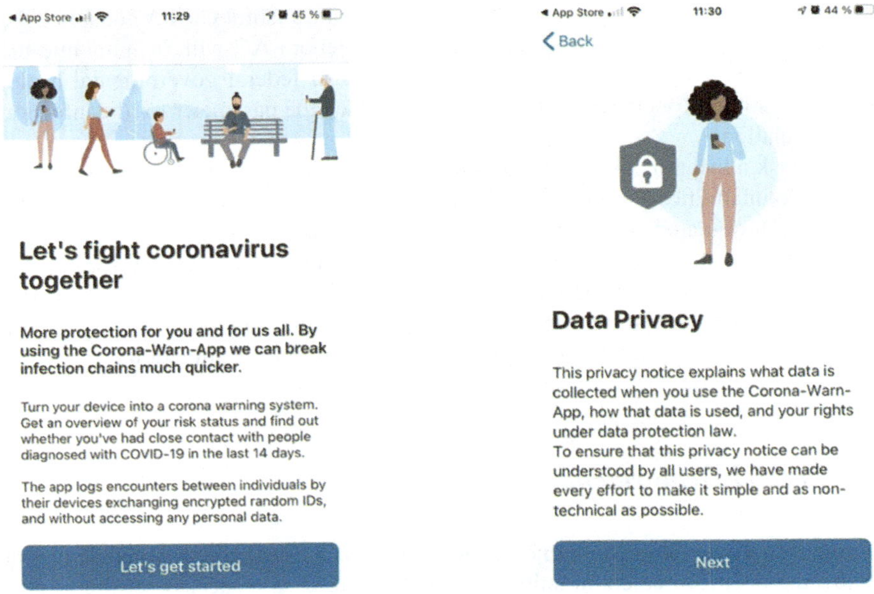

Fig. 3.3 Splash screens 1–2 on initial startup of the app. Screenshot by editor of *Corona-Warn-App* (Version 1.3.0; Robert-Koch-Institut 2020c). Available under Apache 2.0 License at https://github.com/corona-warn-app/cwa-app-ios

Privacy Risk Assessment

In the section "Privacy Concerns", I presented the possible privacy risks of a proximity tracing system that uses BLE. With the Corona-Warn-App's release, I can analyze if and how these risks are still present in the current implementation.

The privacy concerns can be classified into three different types: There concerns regarding (1) exposing personal data like movement data, (2) exposing data about the contact to other people, and (3) exposing medical data. The list of possible privacy breaches is listed in the section "Privacy Concerns".

1. According to the DP-3T teams, the risk of identifying the infected people one encounters is always part of a proximity tracing system. For example, if someone only had contact with a single person on the day the app warns them about, they would know who the infected person is. Because in Germany, the health department already traces and informs the contact persons, the app does not expose additional information. Generally, the solution favors the privacy of the non-infected person over the privacy of the infected person.
2. The Corona-Warn-App uses BLE.
    - The risk to track false contacts via boosted signals is still possible in the German implementation. The risk is part of the distance measurement approach

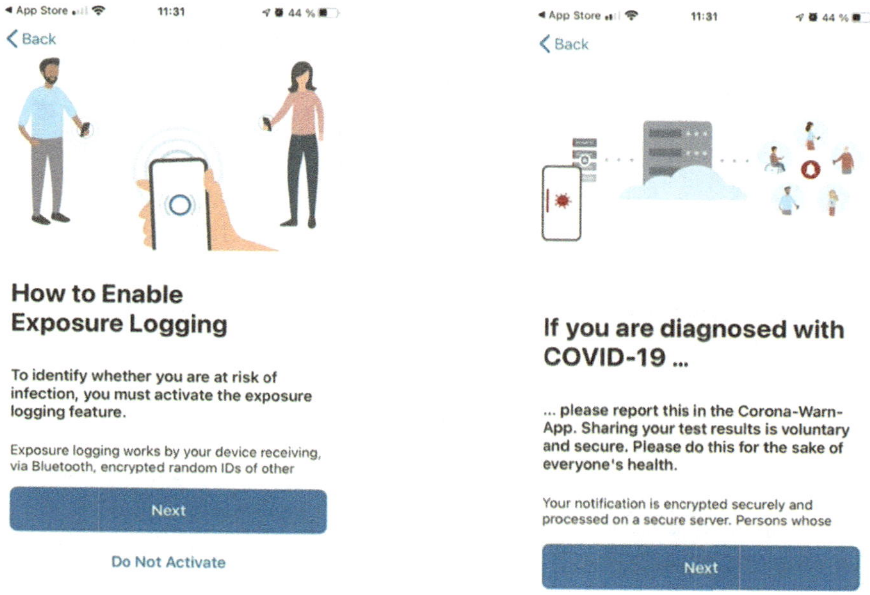

Fig. 3.4 Splash screens 3–4 on initial startup of the app. Screenshot by editor of *Corona-Warn-App* (Version 1.3.0; Robert-Koch-Institut 2020c). Available under Apache 2.0 License at https://github.com/corona-warn-app/cwa-app-ios

of BLE. To avoid this, more data would need to be transmitted between the phones, which in turn would lower the privacy. And even then, it is not guaranteed that this data could not be faked.

- A disruption of the Bluetooth signal is still possible. This is a limitation of the BLE technology.
- The Google and Apple API takes care of randomizing and changing the MAC-Addresses, as well as randomizing and changing the keys.
- It is possible to identify the locations of infected people in hindsight by driving around and gathering keys ("wardriving"). This is still possible in the Corona-Warn-App.

3. The communication with the backend could reveal if a person uses the app or not. The implementation includes a call to the server regardless whether the person revealed a positive test result. Thus, it is not possible to gather information about a positive test result.
4. It can be possible to track the infected persons through their shared keys. This requires scanning the complete area of possible locations in the 14 days prior the message that the person is infected. With the Android and iOS API, the infected

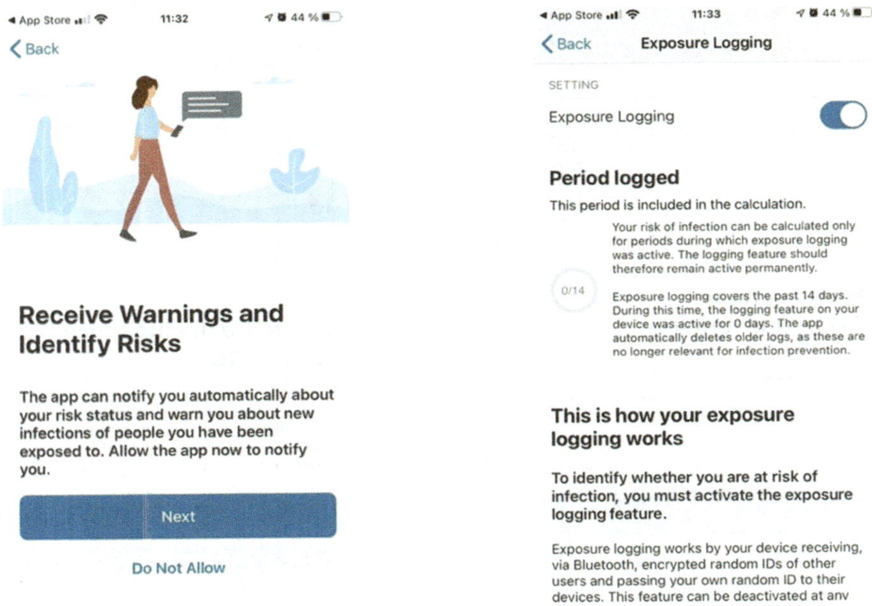

Fig. 3.5 Left: splash screen 5 on initial startup of the app; Right: in-app settings screen. Screenshot by editor of *Corona-Warn-App* (Version 1.3.0; Robert-Koch-Institut 2020c). Available under Apache 2.0 License at https://github.com/corona-warn-app/cwa-app-ios

person shares 14 independent keys, one for each day so the person cannot be tracked for more than a single day. This scanning requires a large effort and could be used to track the person directly. Thus, this breach is considered as acceptable by the DP-3T Team.

5. Irrelevant, since in the implementation the app shares the personal identifiers.

The implementation is not without critics: Contrary to the Corona-Warn-App itself, the API provided by Apple and Google is not open source. Thus, critics argue that any app using the API can also not be considered open source.[1] This is partly because the API interacts with the operating system, and the operating system developers want to protect their trade secrets. A counterargument is that in order to use the app, the user already uses the operating systems and already needs to trust them with their personal data. The API can only be used by trusted government services and is not open to third-party developers. This ensures that it is not used in the background by other programs to spy on the user.

[1]To call a software open source, all parts of the software need to be open source.

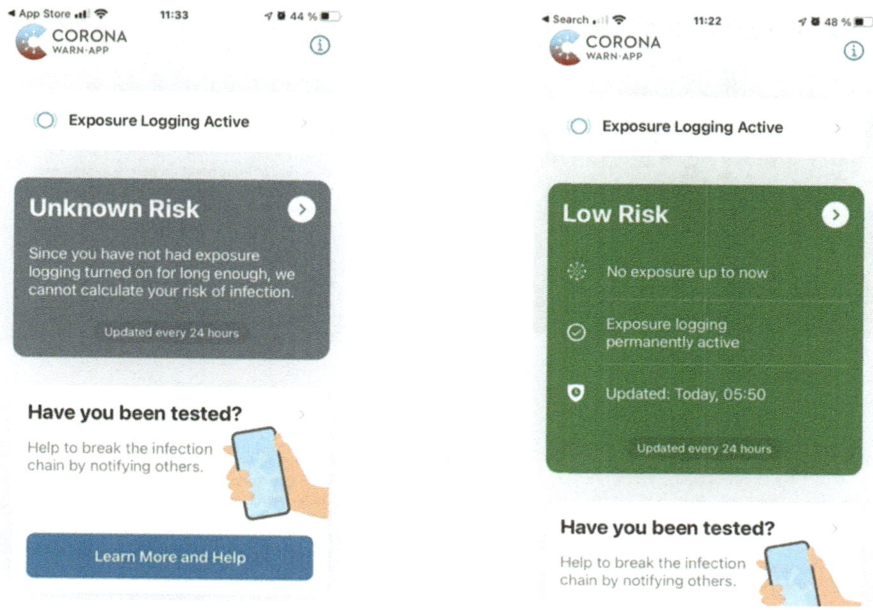

Fig. 3.6 Main screen of the app with different risk assessments. Screenshot by editor of Corona-Warn-App (Version 1.3.0; Robert-Koch-Institut 2020c). Available under Apache 2.0 License at https://github.com/corona-warn-app/cwa-app-ios

Conclusion

The hypothesis formulated in section "Early Solutions of Other Countries" is reflected in a non-peer-reviewed survey by Becker et al. (2020). The authors research the main motivations for and against using a contact tracing app and how they are influenced. The main points against using a contact tracing app are, when the app uses location and medical data, and when the app exposes the identity of the user. Positive motivations can be reached, if the usage of the app helps with lifting regional restrictions (not specifically for the users).

An interesting observation is that the long discussion in the German media about the privacy risks of the contact tracing app did not influence the motivation to install the app (Becker et al. 2020). But, in hindsight, it helped independent experts to influence the development of the app. First, it was planned to publish the source code after finishing the development, but after many arguments against this practice the full development was made open source. Additionally, experts and informed user could participate in the development.

An unclear point is the implementation of the app into the healthcare system. Each testing lab in Germany should be able to send the test results through the app. Until now, this is not implemented, and the QR-Code needs to be verified by a phone

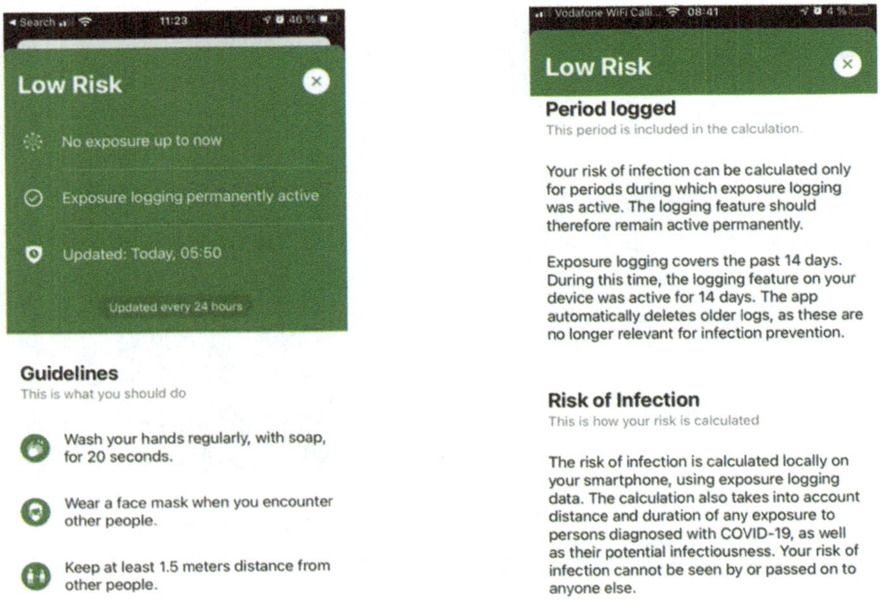

Fig. 3.7 Left: detailed screen with guidelines based on the risk assessment; Right: explaining text. Screenshot by editor of Corona-Warn-App (Version 1.3.0; Robert-Koch-Institut 2020c). Available under Apache 2.0 License at https://github.com/corona-warn-app/cwa-app-ios

hotline. This creates a bottleneck that could cost time during the critical presymptomatic infection phase.

To summarize, the major tool to overcome the challenges before and during the development, was the ability to implement the feedback of independent experts; starting with the decisions to change the architecture from the PEPP-PT to the DP-3T approach, with this changing from a centralized to a decentralized model, and ending with opening the source code during the development and listening to the community feedback.

Future Research Questions and Outlook

A new research area is arising about the practical usefulness of contact tracing apps. Most models that suggest a positive effect do this on basis of a random distribution of installations. But the usage of the app depends on the demographic group. There could be a possible relationship between the usage of the app and abiding to the other measurements for pandemic control. Thus, weakening the impact of the app, because the app has a smaller userbase in the population that is the major driver of the pandemic.

The Australian app failed to catch a single case with a userbase of six million people (as of June 11, 2020), mostly because of overall low case numbers, but also because of the implementation and since most new cases stem from travelers that did not install the app (Bogle 2020). 60% (as of June 29, 2020) of all cases came from overseas transmissions (Ting et al. 2020).

Another point that could drastically reduce the impact of contact tracing apps, is how a high risk level is handled. Currently, exposed people are instructed to avoid possible new infection chains. But especially 'essential workers' are forced to work despite being exposed and their test results still pending. An example are the recent infection clusters at slaughterhouses in NRW with more than 1100 infected people. The workers were pressured to work through extra rent charges for staying at company-provided homes while ill. The pressure to work while ill and in close proximity to others during exhausting physical work in a cold environment accelerated the spread. Thus, it is important to look at how a high-risk level is handled by the stakeholders. The risk levels are provided by the contact tracing through the app or by the health departments. The stakeholders are the exposed people, the employers, the health departments, and the government.

A question for future research could be if it is necessary to provide additional protection by the government for high-risk people. This is especially important for the app because the studies on effectiveness assume that the 'high-risk person' acts according to the instructions and avoids other people.

Also, the psychological effect of the apps can be studied. The usage of the apps could lead people to feel safe regarding COVID-19 and reduce the commitment to the usual pandemic response.

References

Apple. (2020). *Apple und Google arbeiten zusammen an Technologien zur Kontaktverfolgung bei COVID-19*. Retrieved from https://www.apple.com/de/newsroom/2020/04/apple-and-google-partner-on-covid-19-contact-tracing-technology/

Bar-On, Y. M., Flamholz, A., Phillips, R., & Milo, R. (2020). Sars-CoV-2 (COVID-19) by the numbers. *ELife, 9*. https://doi.org/10.7554/eLife.57309.

Becker, K. (2020). *Mit Apps gegen die Pandemie?* Retrieved from https://www.tagesschau.de/inland/coronavirus-forschung-bab-101.html

Becker, S., Degeling, M., Dürmuth, M., Farke, F. M., Schaewitz, L., Schnitzler, T., & Utz, C. (2020). *Akzeptanz von Corona-Apps in Deutschland vor der Einführung der Corona-Warn-App*. Retrieved from Ruhr-Universität Bochum Mobile Security website: https://www.mobsec.ruhr-uni-bochum.de/media/mobsec/veroeffentlichungen/2020/06/29/corona_apps_de1_preprint_de.pdf

Bogle, A. (2020). COVIDSafe has been downloaded by millions, but yet to identify contacts: (and authorities say that's a good thing). *ABC News*. Retrieved from https://www.abc.net.au/news/science/2020-06-11/coronavirus-contact-tracing-app-covid-safe-no-close-contacts/12343138

Dietz, K. (1993). The estimation of the basic reproduction number for infectious diseases. *Statistical Methods in Medical Research, 2*(1), 23–41.

Dominik, K. (2020). Corona-Warn-App Entwicklung: "Architektur der App muss sich kontinuierlich anpassen". *SAP News Germany*. Retrieved from https://news.sap.com/germany/2020/05/corona-warn-app-entwicklung-eyk-kny-thomas-klingbeil/

Ferretti, L., Wymant, C., Kendall, M., Zhao, L., Nurtay, A., Abeler-Dörner, L., & Fraser, C. (2020). Quantifying SARS-CoV-2 transmission suggests epidemic control with digital contact tracing. *Science (New York, N.Y.), 368*(6491). https://doi.org/10.1126/science.abb6936

Frisse, J. (2020). *Zu wenige Menschen nutzen die Corona-Warn-App*. ZEIT ONLINE. Retrieved from https://www.zeit.de/wissen/gesundheit/2020-08/corona-warn-app-contact-tracing-downloads-nutzung-niedrig

German Federal Government. (2020). *Pressekonferenz zur Vorstellung der Corona-Warn-App (Mitschrift im Wortlaut)*. Retrieved from https://www.bundesregierung.de/breg-de/aktuelles/pressekonferenz-zur-vorstellung-der-corona-warn-app-1761058

Greenstone, M., & Nigam, V. (2020). Does social distancing matter? *University of Chicago, Becker Friedman Institute for Economics Working Paper, 2020–26*

Ip, D. K. M., Lau, L. L. H., Leung, N. H. L., Fang, V. J., Chan, K.-H., Chu, D. K. W., & Cowling, B. J. (2017). Viral shedding and transmission potential of asymptomatic and Paucisymptomatic influenza virus infections in the community. *Clinical Infectious Diseases: An Official Publication of the Infectious Diseases Society of America, 64*(6), 736–742. https://doi.org/10.1093/cid/ciw841.

Ministry of Health – Manatū Hauora. (2020). *How NZ COVID tracer works: Use NZ COVID tracer to check in to places you visit by scanning the official Ministry of Health QR codes*. New Zealand. Retrieved from https://www.health.govt.nz/our-work/diseases-and-conditions/covid-19-novel-coronavirus/covid-19-novel-coronavirus-resources-and-tools/nz-covid-tracer-app/how-nz-covid-tracer-works

Norwegian Institute of Public Health. (2020). *Use of Smittestopp and privacy policy*. Norway. Retrieved from https://www.fhi.no/en/id/infectious-diseases/coronavirus/use-of-smittestopp-privacy-policy/

Offenborn, H., & Kolvenbach, M. (2020). *Infizierte nachverfolgen, Datenschutz wahren*. Retrieved from https://www.tagesschau.de/investigativ/swr/tracking-app-101.html

Pfister, J. (2020). *Corona tracker*. Retrieved from https://ctt.pfstr.de/

Robert-Koch-Institut (2020a). *Robert Koch-Institut: COVID-19-Dashboard*. Retrieved from https://experience.arcgis.com/experience/478220a4c454480e823b17327b2bf1d4

Robert-Koch-Institut (2020b). *Tabelle mit Nowcasting-Zahlen zur R-Schätzung*. Retrieved from https://www.rki.de/DE/Content/InfAZ/N/Neuartiges_Coronavirus/Projekte_RKI/Nowcasting_Zahlen.xlsx?__blob=publicationFile

Robert-Koch-Institut. (2020c). *Corona-Warn-App (1.3.0) [Mobile application software]*. Retrieved from https://apps.apple.com/de/app/corona-warn-app/id1512595757?l=en (available under Apache 2.0 license at https://github.com/corona-warn-app/cwa-app-ios)

Tagesschau.de (2020). *Rund 300 Fälle über Warn-App gemeldet*. Retrieved from https://www.tagesschau.de/inland/spahn-corona-app-103.html

Tang, Q. (2020). *Privacy-preserving contact tracing: current solutions and open questions*. Retrieved from http://arxiv.org/pdf/2004.06818v3

The DP-3T Project. (2020). Privacy and security risk evaluation of digital proximity tracing systems. Retrieved from https://github.com/DP-3T/documents/blob/master/Security%20analysis/Privacy%20and%20Security%20Attacks%20on%20Digital%20Proximity%20Tracing%20Systems.pdf

Ting, M., Scott, M., & Workman, M. (2020). Charting the COVID-19 spread in Australia. *ABC News*. Retrieved from https://www.abc.net.au/news/2020-03-17/coronavirus-cases-data-reveals-how-covid-19-spreads-in-australia/12060704?nw=0#newcasesbysource

Troncoso, C. (2020). *Decentralized privacy-preserving proximity tracing: Simplified overview*. Retrieved from https://github.com/DP-3T/documents/blob/master/DP3T%20-%20Simplified%20Three%20Page%20Brief.pdf

Turzer, C. (2020). *Corona-App: Bundesregierung favorisiert dezentralen Ansatz*. WELT. Retrieved from https://www.welt.de/wirtschaft/webwelt/article207509833/Corona-App-Bundesregierung-favorisiert-dezentralen-Ansatz.html

Chapter 4
KidExplore: A New Online Platform to Support Child Development During a Pandemic

Ivan Trilevic

Abstract As a result of the pandemic and the associated lockdown, significant impairments and gaps in educational and developmental opportunities for children are becoming increasingly apparent. This results in the need for innovative, digital educational concepts to support children's development, which is the subject and purpose of this essay. The source material used for this essay consists mainly of scientific journals from the fields of information systems (IS) and economics. In addition, a survey was conducted to identify the problems and requirements of the stakeholders. Based on this, the concept for *KidExplore* was developed, which is an online platform that provides access to countless children's activities with just one subscription membership. Thereby, the platform on the one hand enables children to participate in a wide variety of different online courses and on the other hand helps course providers mastering the pandemic through digitalization.

Keywords Pandemic · Child development · Online courses for children · Online platform · Subscription membership

Introduction

The world stands still as the COVID-19 pandemic surprised society. As of August 2020, over 900,000 people have died (World Health Organization 2020), millions of people are in lockdown, and education as well as workplaces have moved online as far as possible. As a consequence, the existence of many companies is threatened, many companies may not survive the pandemic on their own means and are looking for help. The COVID-19 pandemic has shown that many businesses are not prepared for digitalization and do not have a backup plan for a situation like this. A quick reaction is necessary by adapting as many companies as possible to the new

I. Trilevic (✉)
University of Cologne, Cologne, Germany
e-mail: itrilevi@smail.uni-koeln.de

C. Hovestadt et al. (eds.), *Digital Responses to Covid-19*, SpringerBriefs in Information Systems, https://doi.org/10.1007/978-3-030-66611-8_4

circumstances: Digital technologies received a significant focus as they can provide the means for mastering the crisis. Especially in times of lockdown, digitalization is the best solution to ensure that business can continue. This also manifests in statistics: According to the Frick (2019), only 9% of all entrepreneurs emerge stronger from a crisis; however, companies that have primarily focused on digital transformation emerge stronger than others.

The pandemic also impacts the mental health and wellbeing of adults as well as children. The reasons for the impairment include lack of support, trauma and unhelpful thinking styles (Roddick 2016). Children, in particular, absorb the wellbeing of caregivers at a young age (Newland 2015). Experts in behavioral health propose a five-dimension model of wellbeing in children: social, physical, emotional, intellectual, and spiritual (Kids Harbor 2020). Throughout the pandemic, people are increasingly dependent on digital technology to learn, live, and stay connected (Goldschmidt 2020). Digital technology may be used to leverage and maintain the wellbeing of children even more by moving activities for children online that can no longer take place in the physical world due to pandemic countermeasures. This would help children who would otherwise stagnate in their development because they have reduced opportunities to learn new skills and because they have no connection to other children, which means that the social component in particular is lacking.

One of the most important factors in such a crisis situation is to protect the health of employees and children in order to fight the pandemic. This requires creative measures and is ultimately a matter of taking advantage of opportunities and adopting fast. On that basis, the research question of this essay is: How can children continue to participate in education in times of a pandemic without a risk of infection?

The goal of this essay is therefore to develop a concept on how children may continue to participate in educational courses during a pandemic without a risk of infection. A second goal of the concept is to help course providers to secure the existence of their companies during the pandemic. Third, the concept should provide extension points for future development.

Tackling the problems posed by the pandemic can potentially mitigate the impact of the crisis and may be a long-term alternative after the pandemic has ended. This essay will offer a detailed proposal of how a concept can support the economy as well as child health and continuous child development.

Related Work

For the search of related literature, a search string has been developed. It is composed of clusters of synonyms for (i) "pandemic", (ii) "children", and (iii) "digital technology". The search string has been applied to find papers in several leading scholarly research journals from the information systems (IS) and economics fields.

The results are reviewed in this section. All in all, only a small number of meaningful literature could be found using the search string above. This was predictable, as the respective topics only started to gain relevance since the start of the pandemic.

Drane (2020) examine in their paper that mass school closures have the risk of reinforcing existing educational inequities. Children need a sense of stability during a sudden change to help them process, adjust and develop new strategies for coping with emerging and fluid contexts. For many, schools provide that stability.

Esposito et al. (2020) describe that school closures can cause the deepening of social, economic and health inequities. Nevertheless, distance learning and exercising using digital technologies to replace traditional schooling can be hard to implement as every child must have the necessary hard- and software available for them to use. A 2015 survey in Italy showed that, in the poorest areas of the country, 41% of households had no tablet or computer. Only 14.3% of households with at least one child could provide the prerequisites for distance learning (Istituto Nazionale di Statistica 2015). This leads Esposito et al. (2020) to conclude "that a relevant group of children may remain substantially excluded not only from learning but also from any form of socialization with peers and with the surrounding world."

Goldschmidt (2020) deals with the topic how digital technology became essential during a time of isolation and social distancing. The author discusses the aforementioned five dimensions for the wellbeing of children identified by behavioral health experts: social, physical, emotional, intellectual, and spiritual wellbeing. She concludes that as a result of the pandemic, "the digital divide is more apparent than ever" (Goldschmidt 2020), as children today know how to use computers, while instructors and teaching methods are often behind and need to catch up. Still, new educational models would be created out of necessity. Nowadays the internet is commonplace, since an "access to a computer is as essential for learning in school as is owning paper, pencils and books." (Goldschmidt 2020). Due to the fact that still not every household has a computer, the author calls for a solution in partnership of government, businesses, and educational institutions (Goldschmidt 2020).

Based on the literature that has been reviewed, a potential concept has been developed to enable children and companies that offer courses for children to continue offering courses online in times of crisis. This would enable an exchange of information and mitigate the restrictions in social contact. In addition, children would have the flexibility to try out different courses and creativity would be encouraged. The fact that the courses take place online means that the risk of infection through participation in the courses is eliminated. Finally, companies offering courses for children would be able to resume their business, which in the best-case scenario could ensure the existence of these companies.

Analysis and Concept Development

Business Idea/Product

The current state of the art in the sphere of children's course providers is usually based on physical courses and has not yet been shaped by digitalization. Many children's course providers in Germany have ignored digitalization and often do not even have a website. As a result, the establishment of a digital course booking system as well as the practice of online marketing for the purpose of acquiring new customers is a long way off. But what already exists on the German market is a website where the most important information about course providers is stored. This website is called *Kidsgo*. In the city of Cologne alone, Kidsgo lists more than 1000 children courses and in Berlin far more than 2000.

In order to change this situation and to help children's course providers with their digitalization, the *KidExplore* concept was created as a result of this project. The concept's goal is to digitalize children's courses and to offer children an opportunity to develop their interests freely even during the pandemic and thus promote their development during this difficult time. The project is carried out in an innovative way and creates a new business model that should be profitable for all parties involved.

KidExplore is an online platform that provides access to countless children's activities with just one subscription membership, thereby enabling children to participate in almost all online courses in a wide range of topics. The membership offers variety and flexibility and differs from classic membership models such multiple-unit tickets, semester fees, and annual memberships, that are only valid for one specific course and are binding. Since children discover many new interests and preferences in their early development, KidExplore makes it possible to develop and support these interests online during pandemics without being tied to several memberships in which the children often lose interest after a while and thus the membership is not fully utilized.

Through a website and a native smartphone app, courses can easily be found, categorized, filtered, and booked online, independent of time and place. KidExplore's offer consists of courses offered by third-party course providers, who can now shift their physical business into location-independent digital business by using the KidExplore video conferencing system. They can use the platform as an additional distribution channel and thus generate an additional source of income. Course providers benefit from the innovative online course booking procedure, which is based on a credit system. They can thus actively optimize and scale their business with digital online marketing. The online presence on the platform expands the customer base of the course and reaches new interest groups (target groups).

In order to predict potential problems the involved stakeholders—such as children, parents, or course providers—might have with a subscription-based membership model, it was first necessary to crystallize their most important pain points and needs. Therefore, an online survey has been carried out: It survey was aimed at parents who, together with their child, evaluated data on the children's participation behavior in leisure, sports, and cultural activities. The survey collected responses from 16 participants (parents with children), more than ¾ of the interviewees stated that the process of finding a suitable course is mainly carried out via the internet and recommendations from close acquaintances. Twelve stated that they had already specifically searched for courses on the internet but had missed a browsing function to get inspired and discover new activities. The survey also revealed that 10 of the children had not attended a course in full at some point and therefore the memberships their parents had payed for was not fully utilized. This may result from the curiosity and the dynamic interests of each child in development. In addition, parents on the one hand often do not know what numerous possible activities there are for their children to participate in, since only a few children activities have an internet presence or advertising. On the other hand, many children's activities have binding contracts, for which the parents pay annual membership fees. Children are very curious at a young age and want to try out many things, develop new interests and preferences. It can be like that a child participates in one course in one week which they liked and in the next week the child would like to do something completely different. In this scenario the parents have now payed for the one course and the child is no longer interested in it.

KidExplore aims to solve this by offering children to participate in countless children's activities in a wide range of categories with just one membership that can be canceled monthly. Using the website or the mobile app, parents can find all the children's courses, and filter them by age, interests, ratings, and time. Courses can be booked directly and can be attended interactively using the built-in video conferemcing system. On the basis of the courses booked, members are suggested courses individually, which correspond to the preferences of the child. By becoming a member of KidExplore, digital coins are credited monthly to the member's account. These coins are available to members to book any course. Each course will have an individual value, which has been determined in advance with the course provider.

A further advantage for the online course providers is that the cooperation, promotion and the platform's digital tools are free of charge. Course providers get free marketing through KidExplore (social media, newsletter etc.) which gives courses reach and every time a course is booked, income is generated for the course provider. Through the partner page, the course providers have an overview of when and on which days the course has been booked. This makes it easier to scale and adapt courses. In addition, the course providers can see the monthly income generated by the individual courses, which they will receive from KidExplore on a monthly basis. This saves the course provider the administrative work of registering and deregistering children and billing the parents.

Customers

KidExplore has two groups of customers: First, there are parents and their children, who want to use a digital flexible membership during the pandemic, which does not contractually bind them to only one course at a time. Second, there are course providers of children activities in all categories, who want to have their course offers digitalized, want to gain new customers, have free marketing, and be relieved of administrative work.

KidExplore's main selling points in comparison to other providers are the following:

1. The onboarding process for new online course providers can be carried out fully automatically in just a few steps via a special partner tool. The course provider only needs a regular computer.
2. The online course providers have no costs when using KidExplore. This includes the partner tool using which courses can be easily scaled. The course providers get an exact overview of visitor numbers, sales, as well as statistics on the visits (age, gender, target group).
3. KidExplore offers parents and their children, compared to other providers, a membership for all courses.

The surveys and discussions with 16 parents and their children in the last month have shown that both parents and course providers are convinced of the KidExplore business model. Parents are in favor of paying for just one membership with which their children can participate in all online courses offered by KidExplore and not being bound to different memberships. They also appreciate the possibility to find all available courses on the website or in the smartphone app and to book them directly online. On the other hand, course providers welcome the opportunity to survive an economically difficult time and to receive free marketing through the KidExplore web app as well as the possibility to reach new target groups through the platform.

Conclusion

Summary

In summary, the COVID-19 pandemic is resulting in enormous economic difficulties for children's course providers. The absence of digitalization in this industry is now becoming increasingly noticeable, forcing course providers to take action. Since the revenue is declining sharply or is even non-existent during this period, the course providers are faced with the problem of expensive digital upgrades. For many this is financially unviable, while facing existential threats as long as the pandemic goes on. KidExplore offers the them a platform to digitalize their courses. This also brings many advantages for the course providers, such as a free online presence, the expansion of their customer base, and a free booking software.

On the other hand, KidExplore offers children the valuable opportunity to continue to participate digitally in pedagogically valuable children's courses during the pandemic and not to stagnate in their development. On the contrary, they can now discover and develop new interests without being financially burdened to their parents, who would else be forced to subscribe to long-term memberships.

Outlook

After the pandemic, KidExplore can continue to maintain their online product variety and expand their product range to local classroom courses in the future. In addition to their coverage of the online sector, an expansion to the physical presence sector would be possible. Course providers can continue to take advantage of the many benefits of the service and focus on their core business of course execution. KidExplore represents another lucrative source of income and extends the reach for new customer acquisition.

References

Drane, C. (2020). *The impact of 'learning at home' on the educational outcomes of vulnerable children in Australia during the COVID-19 pandemic*. National Centre for Student Equity in Higher Education.

Esposito, et al. (2020). School closure during the coronavirus disease 2019 (COVID-19) pandemic: An effective intervention at the global level? *JAMA Pediatrics, 174*, 921.

Frick, W. (2019). How to survive a recession and thrive afterward. *Harvard Business Review, 97*(3), 98–105.

Goldschmidt, K. (2020). The COVID-19 pandemic: Technology use to support the wellbeing of children. *Journal of Pediatric Nursing, 53*, 88–90.

Harvard Business Review. (2019, May–June). How to survive a recession and thrive afterward. *Category Economics & Society*. Retrieved from https://hbr.org/2019/05/how-to-survive-a-recession-and-thrive-afterward

Istituto Nazionale di Statistica. (2015). *Italy in figures 2015*. Retrieved from https://www.istat.it/en/files/2015/09/ItalyinFigures2015.pdf

Kids Harbor. (2020). *Teaching children about wellness: 5 areas of focus*. Retrieved from https://www.kids-harbor.com/teaching-children-about-wellness/

Newland, L. (2015). Family wellbeing, parenting, and child well-being: Pathways to health adjustment. *Clinical Psychologist, 19*, 3–14.

Roddick, M. (2016). Eight dimensions of wellbeing: Where do you fit it? *Good Therapy*. Retrieved from https://www.goodtherapy.org/blog/8-dimensions-of-wellbeing-where-do-you-fit-in-0527164

World Health Organization. (2020). *WHO Coronavirus disease (COVID-19) dashboard*. Retrieved from https://covid19.who.int

Chapter 5
Digital Tools for Digital Natives: Learning in Times of a Global Pandemic

Simon Friedrich Murillo

Abstract COVID-19 caused a global pandemic that is responsible for severe changes in our daily lives, including the education sector, which shifted from a face-to-face environment to less supervised learning from home. This chapter presents the role of digital tools for digital natives and their role in support of learning during the global pandemic. After an overview of existing approaches and current articles on COVID-19 in which the challenges of this special time are explained, I suggest that changes to our educational system are needed in order to prepare the next generation for the challenges that are yet to come. Virtual schools are one way forward in order to prepare teachers, students, and parents in using and benefiting from digital tools. It is also emphasized that more research is needed in the area of gamification and how digital tools can be used in a demand-oriented way.

Keywords Digital natives · Virtual school · e-Learning · Motivation · COVID-19

Introduction

COVID-19 caused a global pandemic that is responsible for severe changes to our daily lives and presents new challenges to our society. For example, travel restrictions, social distancing guidelines and quarantine actions limit individual choices. In most European countries, schools and kindergartens have been closed to further limit the number of social contacts. Yet, this puts an additional burden on parents when working from home.

In many countries, different approaches to resuming school and teaching operations have been implemented. While some approaches advocate that high school graduates should be the first to return to school so that they can prepare for their final exams, other countries, such as Denmark or France, have made it possible for younger students to return to school first, in order to help parents continue their

---

S. Friedrich Murillo (✉)
University of Cologne, Cologne, Germany

C. Hovestadt et al. (eds.), *Digital Responses to Covid-19*, SpringerBriefs in Information Systems, https://doi.org/10.1007/978-3-030-66611-8_5

employment (Schmidt 2020). Other countries seek to strike the balance by having students partly taught online (from home), so that others can be taught in classroom in line with social distancing guidelines. This means that students not only have to follow lessons online, but also that they must carry out many activities such as learning or homework independently at home.

While there is ample research on how students can be successfully taught in school, there is still a lack of research on the motivation of students to learn independently from home. Digital tools provide manifold opportunities in motivating students. Such tools can support students in achieving learning success even without physical presence in a classroom. Hence, I seek to answer the following research question:

> What digital tools support student's independent learning from home?

In order to answer this research question, I start by giving an overview of existing approaches that advocate the use of digital tools for education. I will also include current articles and use cases considering COVID-19, explaining the challenges of this particular time. The results summarize old and novel uses of digital tools already available that help address the unique needs of the global pandemic. I conclude this chapter with a discussion of the implications for research and practice.

Existing Approaches for the Use of Digital Tools for Education

Related work can be divided into three areas. First, prior literature proposed and investigated the concept of a virtual school. Second, prior scholars have suggested the use of games in education. Third, prior literature has already accumulated evidence and knowledge on computer-based learning tools. I discuss each area in turn.

The Virtual School

Online learning and teaching are nothing new. Rather, it is and has been practiced in many rural regions. A prior review article summarized the core advantages and disadvantages of virtual schools (Barbour and Reeves 2009). One of the most frequently cited benefit is the *expanding educational access*, which means that smaller and rural schools can offer courses for which they would otherwise not have sufficient staff and capacity. A second important advantage are *further learning opportunities*. Online courses offer students more opportunities, such as email or discussion forums, to interact with the teacher and other students. Also, shy students are given the necessary "thinking time" to participate in the conversation (Tinker and Haavind 1996). Other studies investigate teachers migration from a classroom to an online classroom and back (Lowes 2008). Such migration can change the teacher's personal teaching practice in subtle and important ways. Most of the positive changes reported by teachers involved the *course redesign* itself, whether it was adding units from the online course or eliminating lessons that appeared poorly designed. Another benefit is that students and teachers alike *learn important technological skills* that not only increase individual marketability but also facilitate access to information and resources that are becoming increasingly important in our digital world (Donlevy 2003). The *increase in effectiveness* in administrative tasks such as registration, attendance and grading or the *flexibility in scheduling* for students and teachers are two additional advantages of virtual schools that have been proposed by prior literature (Keeler 2003).

However, the disadvantages of virtual schools should not be neglected. For example, numerous studies show that the only students who are typically successful in online learning environments are those who are highly motivated by themselves and who have strong time management, literacy and technological skills (Barbour and Reeves 2009). These characteristics are those typically associated with adult learners and may not apply to all younger students. Opportunities for social and emotional learning normally arise from interpersonal contact in the classroom, yet these are unavailable in an online classroom (Donlevy 2003). Disadvantaged students in particular tend to benefit more from a school with adults who can provide the emotional support that these students often do not receive at home (Morgan 2015). Recent work examines the challenges of the transition to digitized education within the COVID-19 crisis and found that in particular insufficient and inexperienced teachers, have hindered the success of education in this process (Kayalar 2020).

In sum, we can benefit from technological advances in order to compensate for environmental disruptions, but we need to support people that may lack the technological skills in order to benefit from these advances.

The Gamification of Education

A second relevant stream of literature investigates the use of video games for enhanced learning experience. Video games are known for tapping into individual's motivation in order to enhance engagement and playtime. For example, Minecraft has be used in education and research (Nebel et al. 2016). The games' simple game mechanics and comprehensive modification tools offer a whole range of possible uses. Players can use the game to develop different skillsets. Examples include engineering skills, when building houses and even entire cities, creative skills, when designing new artifacts, exploration, when investigating the virtual world. Minecraft and related serious games can be very helpful in combining individuals' motivation with new learning experiences. However, since related courses are often electives limiting the number of student's participation. In addition, many serious games have hardware and software requirements and hence, their use is often limited to the school's infrastructure.

However, when design features of video games are used in order to improve software, the literature refers to the term gamification (Morschheuser et al. 2018). Gamification has drawn a lot of attention, as it seeks to benefit from the motivational elements used in video game design for accomplishing other, typically mundane tasks. A review on gamification and learning, highlights the notion of using game functions (elements, mechanics, frames, aesthetics, thinking, metaphors) in non-game settings (Faiella and Ricciardi 2015). However, the study suggests a lack of experimental studies on the use of game elements in educational processes. As a result, it is difficult to judge the effectiveness and usefulness of applying gamification to improve learning experiences and learning outcomes. Certain characteristics of gamification can also have negative effects on motivation (Faiella and Ricciardi 2015), such as social comparison within an e-learning course as some students may not want to compete with their classmates (Domínguez et al. 2013). Therefore, it is important to examine specific elements of gamification rather than gamification alone as an overarching concept (Hanus and Fox 2015). Another study compared different gaming features, showing that the use of adaptive gaming functions can increase motivation amongst the most engaged learners (Lavoue et al. 2019).

In sum, serious games and gamification give us a toolkit to enhance learning experiences and learning outcome by tapping into student's motivation, yet more studies are needed in order better understand the performance implications.

Computer-Based Learning Tools

There are many support tools to help learner's complete homework and prepare for exams, using different approaches. However, many of these systems do not take into account how students manage their work (Mendicino et al. 2009). Students may be less organized when managing their tasks or carrying out their activities outside of school. Especially for the latter, the teacher is less likely to find the cause of a problem as when the students are being taught in person. Therefore, it is important to integrate formal (e.g., the lessons of a teacher in an online or non-online classroom), non-formal (e.g., an interest group outside the formal learning environment) and informal (e.g., those provided by individuals in family or friends rather than the teacher) environments to achieve best learning outcomes (Radović and Passey 2016). A review of computer-based assessment identified several important points to consider when assessing learning performance (Shute and Rahimi 2017). For example, feedback should be given in manageable units (Shute 2008) and should be designed so that students actually use it and do not ignore it (Maier et al. 2016). Also, well designed and elaborated feedback is more helpful than simple verification feedback (Rodrigues and Oliveira 2014). Digital tools can improve learning in a number of content areas. For example, tools can keep students in touch with the course material, allowing them to monitor their progress in the course (Shute and Rahimi 2017). Also, self-regulatory skills can be supported by encouraging students to be attentive and reflective when responding to questions in a web-based assessment system for learning, which in turn can improve learning (Wang 2011). In addition, a positive correlation between the use of web-based tools and students' performance in standardized tests has been demonstrated (Koedinger et al. 2010; Wang 2011). However, the use of digital learning technologies can increase the performance gap (Bjerede and Krueger 2015) caused by differences in their learning environment at home.

In sum, digital tools help good teachers to improve the cognitive skills and performance of their students but has the opposite effect for unskilled teachers.

Digital Tools for the Education of Digital Natives: An Analysis of the Literature

Shortly after the turn of the millennium, the terms Digital Native and Digital Immigrants gained popularity as Prensky (2001) pointing out that the needs of modern students are not being met by the current education system. Apart from this, digitalization is having an increasing impact on our daily lives and changing the way we work, live and learn. It provides us with many new opportunities and challenges. The COVID-19 pandemic has led to the increased adoption of distance learning and has revealed the impact and status of digital technologies in different countries. While, there is also ample evidence suggesting that digital technologies can be successfully used for homework, learning or teaching with positive motivation and performance implications, there is also much evidence for the careless use of such digital technologies can also lead to greater inequality or even a reduction in performance.

Inequality in access to and use of information and communication technologies between individuals in different socio-economic conditions—that is, the digital gap—has become more visible (Kayalar 2020). For example, parents' education, access to resources (e.g., computers and applications), or even gender can have a negative impact on home schooling inequality during the COVID-19 pandemic (Bol 2020). It is clear that our educational systems must adapt to our digitized world in order to prepare future generations for these challenges. The way we learn is changing through the use of digital technologies and we must prepare our student to take full advantage of their benefits. In the following, I discuss the available approaches using digital tools and their implications toward students learning (see Table 5.1).

One of the best approaches I have found during my research are virtual schools. In particular, I mean that schools participating in a virtual school program acquire the necessary know-how to slowly prepare teachers for the use of digital tools. For example, future professional development for teachers may prioritize a

Table 5.1 Overview of approaches, benefits and exemplary solutions

Approach	Benefits	Exemplary solution
Virtual schools	Teachers and students acquire needed skills to use digital tools	edu.google.com (Google suite for EDU)
In-service training	Improves quality of online teaching. Supports virtual school	Creativeschools.eu
Apps	Good learning opportunity. Uses mobile technology	Simpleclub.com
Assignment quizzes	Allows students to focus on learning	Kahoot.com
Gamification	Supports the development of new learning apps	Seppo.io
Tablet PC's	Easily attach picture to homework assignments. Improves communication	Apple iPad or Amazon Fire HD

comprehensive communication strategy between schools and families before remote learning begins (Clausen et al. 2020). In its study, Clausen et al. (2020) also suggests which communication tools can be used (e.g., Google Suite for Education: a variety of tools and resources for family engagement; Audacity: audio recording tool for creating podcasts or announcements) in order to improve communication and reduce the homework-gap. Lowes (2008) has found in her research that the requirement to make a certain amount of posts a week or to respond to student posts can increase student participation. Such procedures should be taught by teachers and students in the future, but without using such novel tools, learning success cannot occur.

Kayalar (2020) concludes that **in-service training** for beginners and inexperienced teachers is extremely important for dealing with online education. The principle of the Virtual High School can not only help teachers to teach better and make the learning offer more flexible, but also helps to move the teaching offer completely online, as it is necessary now in the time of the pandemic. Another advantage of virtual schools is that they can enable small or rural schools in particular to offer high quality courses that they would otherwise not be able to provide due to a lack of resources. This, in turn, can increase motivation as it allows students a wider choice of courses and allows them to choose subjects they are much more interested in (Barbour and Reeves 2009).

Of course there are also other good learning opportunities and **Apps** (e.g., simpleclub.com in Germany) which promise high motivation and learning success by cleverly combining digital technologies such as Apps with integrated videos, quizzes or PDF summaries of various courses ("Simpleclub," 2020), but not everyone has the necessary knowledge or technical understanding to use such opportunities and not everyone can afford such an offer, which can lead to greater inequality in society.

A further approach by D. E. Schmidt, Sanchez, and Dickerson (2017) is to replace homework with **assignment quizzes**. This method was motivated by the belief that providing reference material allows students to shift their focus and energy from searching for solutions to engaging the solution process thus enabling them to operate within a higher cognitive domain—shifting from understanding to application, analysis and evaluation (Schmidt et al. 2017).

Gamification is also an important tool to increase the motivation of students and is partly used in the above-mentioned learning apps. However, there are not enough scientific studies dealing with specific elements of gamification and focusing them on learning success for as many students as possible.

It has already been shown that the use of **Tablet PCs**, for example, has several advantages when doing homework, such as the ability to quickly correct mistakes or attach pictures or comments to improve communication between teachers and students (Dicken 2008). Unfortunately, experiments like this one, which was conducted at an independent school where any student can lease a Tablet PC, are not (or not yet) applicable to general education systems.

Table 5.1 summarizes the different digital tools for the education of digital natives that have been discussed and also outlines exemplary implementations available already today.

Discussion

The schooling system has so far been largely physical in nature, more often digital tools have been introduced and used in higher education institutions. Still, many learnings can be drawn from these experiences. Our younger generations are growing up as digital natives, yet we have not yet harnessed all the benefits digital tools provide when educating our younger generation.

Based on my review of the literature, I suggest that fundamental changes to our educational system are needed in order to prepare the next generation for the challenges that are yet to come. Virtual schools are one way forward in order to prepare teachers, students and parents in using and benefiting from digital tools. As we progress, we need to treat carefully in order to ensure that technological advances do not widen the digital gap. More research is needed in order to provide solutions overcoming these societal challenges. This is also in line with the findings of the Barbour and Reeves (2009) study, which states that the virtual school movement continues to grow and serving a wider range of students, creating an urgent need for more and better research that can help ensure that all students have the opportunity to succeed in virtual school environments.

Also, more research is needed that showcases the benefit of gamification in supporting students to do their homework and in motivating students to learn. Of particular interest is the questions about design elements that help increase learning effects on a larger scale. This is particularly important in order to prepare for future disaster scenarios. In such scenarios, we need to develop solutions that provide safe learning environments for students without restricting access to few selective students based on their access to technology.

Conclusion

Education during the pandemic has been highly dependent on parents-as-teachers. Schools must claim back a more pronounced role by ensuring equal learning opportunities through means available in a digitalized world. Students who grow up in households where the use of technology is limited or where parents can only offer limited after-school support, academic achievement may not be valued. Such lack of valuations for some and high valuation for others represent a gap in our society. This gap puts students whose parents are supportive and technologically literate at an advantage over those who do not receive support (Bjerede and Krueger 2015). However, an expansion of virtual schools can help close this gap, providing equal opportunities to all our students.

One of the biggest barriers during the COVID-19 pandemic was that teachers were not prepared for the switch to online courses. They were overwhelmed by the transition from physical to digital classrooms (Gewertz 2020). Teachers were faced with a variety of challenges, such as acquiring technical skills, developing new teaching concepts, and findings new ways to grade homework. They were flooded with e-mails, texts and phone calls from school directors, parents and students, who were also overwhelmed by the situation. At the same time teachers had to deal with unfamiliar technologies themselves. Many challenges would have been less severe if technical skills and experience in online courses had been available. However, the adaption of virtual courses now prepares the participants for the future. It also provides students and teachers with important technological skills that increase individual marketability and facilitates access to information and resources (Donlevy 2003). Digital skills are needed by our students who wish to succeed in the academic or business world, given the fundamental aspect of digital technologies.

References

Barbour, M. K., & Reeves, T. C. (2009). The reality of virtual schools: A review of the literature. *Computers & Education, 52*(2), 402–416.

Bjerede, M., & Krueger, K. R. (2015). How digital equity can help close the homework gap. *THE Journal (Technological Horizons in Education), 42*(5).

Bol, T. (2020). *Inequality in homeschooling during the Corona crisis in the Netherlands*. First results from the LISS Panel.

Clausen, J. M., Bunte, B. L., & Robertson, E. T. (2020). Professional development to improve communication and reduce the homework gap in grades 7-12 during COVID-19 transition to remote learning. *Journal of Technology and Teacher Education, 28*(2).

Dicken, C. (2008). The 30-day challenge: Digital homework in a high school mathematics classroom. In *The impact of tablet PCs and pen-based technology on education: Evidence and outcomes*.

Domínguez, A., Saenz-de-Navarrete, J., de-Marcos, L., Fernández-Sanz, L., Pagés, C., & Martínez-Herráiz, J.-J. (2013). Gamifying learning experiences: Practical implications and outcomes. *Computers & Education, 63*, 380–392.

Donlevy, J. (2003). Teachers, technology and training: Online learning in virtual high school. *International Journal of Instructional Media, 22*(2).

Faiella, F., & Ricciardi, M. (2015). Gamification and learning: A review of issues and research. *Journal of E-Learning and Knowledge Society, 11*(3).

Gewertz, C. (2020). Exhausted and grieving: Teaching during the coronavirus crisis. *Education Week, 39(30)*. Retrieved from https://www.edweek.org/ew/articles/2020/04/16/exhausted-and-grieving-teaching-during-the-coronavirus.html

Hanus, M. D., & Fox, J. (2015). Assessing the effects of gamification in the classroom: A longitudinal study on intrinsic motivation, social comparison, satisfaction, effort, and academic performance. *Computers & Education, 80*, 152–161.

Kayalar, F. (2020). Shift to digitalized education due to Covid-19 pandemic and the difficulties the teachers encountered in the process. In *Proceedings of the Multidisciplinary Academic Conference*.

Keeler, C. G. (2003). Developing and using an instrument to describe instructional design elements of high school online courses.

Koedinger, K. R., McLaughlin, E. A., & Heffernan, N. T. (2010). A quasi-experimental evaluation of an on-line formative assessment and tutoring system. *Journal of Educational Computing Research, 43*(4), 489–510.

Lavoue, E., Monterrat, B., Desmarais, M., & George, S. (2019). Adaptive gamification for learning environments. *IEEE Transactions on Learning Technologies, 12*(1), 16–28.

Lowes, S. (2008). Online teaching and classroom change: The trans-classroom teacher in the age of the internet. *Innovate: Journal of Online Education, 4*(3).

Maier, U., Wolf, N., & Randler, C. (2016). Effects of a computer-assisted formative assessment intervention based on multiple-tier diagnostic items and different feedback types. *Computers & Education, 95*, 85–98.

Mendicino, M., Razzaq, L., & Heffernan, N. T. (2009). A comparison of traditional homework to computer-supported homework. *Journal of Research on Technology in Education, 41*(3), 331–359.

Morgan, H. (2015). Online instruction and virtual schools for middle and high school students: Twenty-first-century fads or progressive teaching methods for today's pupils? *The Clearing House: A Journal of Educational Strategies, Issues and Ideas, 88*(2), 72–76.

Morschheuser, B., Hassan, L., Werder, K., & Hamari, J. (2018). How to design gamification? A method for engineering gamified software. *Information and Software Technology, 95*, 219–237.

Nebel, S., Schneider, S., & Rey, G. D. (2016). Mining learning and crafting scientific experiments: A literature review on the use of minecraft in education and research. *Educational Technology & Society, 19*(2).

Prensky, M. (2001). Digital natives, Digital immigrants Part 1. *On the Horizon, 9*(5).

Radović, S., & Passey, D. (2016). Digital resource developments for mathematics education involving homework across formal, non-formal and informal settings. *The Curriculum Journal, 27*(4), 538–559.

Rodrigues, F., & Oliveira, P. (2014). A system for formative assessment and monitoring of students' progress. *Computers & Education, 76*, 30–41.

Schmidt, H. (2020). Warum gibt es woanders mehr Unterricht? *Tagesschau*. Retrieved from https://www.tagesschau.de/ausland/schuloeffnungen-101.html

Schmidt, D. E., Sanchez, D. V. P., & Dickerson, S. J. (2017). Increasing student engagement and motivation by replacing homework with assignment-quizzes.

Shute, V. J. (2008). Focus on formative feedback. *Review of Educational Research, 78*(1), 153–189.

Shute, V. J., & Rahimi, S. (2017). Review of computer-based assessment for learning in elementary and secondary education. *Journal of Computer Assisted Learning, 33*(1), 1–19.

Simpleclub. (2020, June 23). Retrieved from https://de.wikipedia.org/wiki/Simpleclub

Tinker, R., & Haavind, S. (1996). Netcourses and netseminars: Current practice and new designs. *Journal of Science Education and Technology, 5*(3), 217–223. https://doi.org/10.1007/BF01575305.

Wang, T.-H. (2011). Developing Web-based assessment strategies for facilitating junior high school students to perform self-regulated learning in an e-Learning environment. *Computers & Education, 57*(2), 1801–1812.

Chapter 6
The Rise of TikTok: The Evolution of a Social Media Platform During COVID-19

Jana Feldkamp

Abstract In the global efforts to fight the pandemic, social distancing guidelines were enforced. Ways to virtually interact and communicate with each other had to be found in order to fulfill social needs. One of these ways were social media platforms as for example TikTok, which download rate increased significantly in the last year. This chapter investigates the rise of TikTok during the global pandemic by reviewing the existing literature from research and practice. As a result, I identified key success factors that supported the rise of TikTok as well as diversification possibilities for the post-pandemic evolution of TikTok. Therefore, the chapter explores the digital transformation of an ecosystem, deriving conceptual knowledge.

Keywords COVID-19 pandemic · COVID-19 lockdown · Social media platform · TikTok

Introduction

#stayathome was a widely used hashtag during the COVID-19 pandemic on different social media platforms (Aerzteblatt 2020). Staying together while being separated seemed to be the slogan for these difficult times. Many countries worldwide imposed quarantines, meaning that millions of people were forced to spend time at home either with their family or alone. Therefore, ways had to be found to survive this new lifestyle of social distancing (LLC 2020). With quarantine measures in place, there was one emerging problem: boredom. Free time activities, hobbies, meeting friends, cultural activities, all these things were no longer possible in order to slow down the spread of the disease.

Given the enforced social distancing guidelines, one thing became clear: the increased role of digital technologies in order to manage the situation. In particular,

J. Feldkamp (✉)
University of Cologne, Cologne, Germany
e-mail: jfeldkam@smail.uni-koeln.de

C. Hovestadt et al. (eds.), *Digital Responses to Covid-19*, SpringerBriefs in Information Systems, https://doi.org/10.1007/978-3-030-66611-8_6

people started communicating and interacting online in order to stay in touch with their social connections. However, many people did not only used the internet to stay in touch with their family and loved once. Many people spent more time on the internet looking for distraction (Johnson 2020a) and recognition. The social isolation as a result of our quarantine measures lead to less recognition, a basic human need (Maslow 1943). Many people were in short-time, work or home office and could not get recognition either from their workplace or their social life. The lack of recognition lead to less motivation for work (Cullinan 2020), creating another problem during the pandemic.

Social media platforms appear to be one solution for both problems resulting of the quarantine measures. These platforms allow users to socially interact with each other, entertain themselves and be recognized, for example when uploading content. Therefore, COVID-19 led to an increased use of digital technologies such as social media platforms. Streaming providers and apps promised distraction and recognition during the pandemic.

Hence, it is not surprising that one big winner of the corona pandemic has been the App TikTok. The download rate of TikTok has increased significantly, so that TikTok was the second most downloaded Android App behind WhatsApp and the most downloaded iOS App in March 2020 (Clement 2020a, b). Between January and March 2020, the app had the best quartal in the Google Play Store and in the Apple Appstore an app ever had and overtook the previous leader "Pokémon Go" (Schwär 2020). TikTok has since become a media phenomenon and with many reports on its success story. Although the app was on the rise even before COVID-19, the corona pandemic acted like a catalyst and fueled the app's reach toward different age groups and regional demographics. Users from all over the world created content on TikTok during the pandemic on various subjects, including the pandemic itself. For example, a Canadian family created the first-ever Quarantine Olympics, doctors used TikTok to convey knowledge about COVID-19 and the song "Bored in the House" of Rapper Tyga went viral because thousands of TikTok users created videos on the song during quarantine (Johnson 2020b).

The increased reach of TikTok and its growing user base lead to more possibilities the platform can develop and pursue. Therefore, this chapter aims to answer the following research question along the example of the app TikTok:

> How did Social Media Platforms evolve due to the COVID-19 pandemic based on the example of TikTok?

Answering this research question helps us to better understand why TikTok was so successful during the corona pandemic and allows us to speculate about the post-pandemic evolution of TikTok.

Background

Social Media Platforms

Social media platforms are mobile and/or internet-based platforms used to facilitate various forms of communication, social interaction, marketing and knowledge-sharing (Obar and Wildman 2015). Famous social media platforms include Facebook, Twitter, and Instagram. While some argue that social media is convoluted, as it may take different forms (Kaplan and Haenlein 2010), others have defined the term as "a web-based service or platform based on web 2.0 technology that enables the sharing, co-creation, discussion and modification of user-generated content" (Werder et al. 2014, p. 3). Carr and Hayes (2015) states that "we know what Social Media are, we are not necessarily able to articulate why they are what they are" (p. 46). Particularly for the younger generations Social Media Platforms become part of their daily routine and social life (Hallikainen 2015).

TikTok is a relatively new social media platform, with the mission to "inspire creativity and bring joy" (TikTok 2020). It is a short-form, video-sharing app that allows users to create and share videos with a length of 15-s and therefore is built around User-generated Content (UGC). Researchers state that one of the main driving forces behind UGC is "self-expression" (Daugherty et al. 2008), "self-enhancement" (Nikolinakou and Phua 2019) and "self-actualization" (Shao 2009). Therefore, users create content on social media platforms to express their thoughts and identity because it may provide them with recognition and fame. Especially in times of socially distancing during corona pandemic, the platforms rich contents have made TikTok immensely popular (Xu et al. 2019).

TikTok Platform Features

One of the most prominent forms of UGC on TikTok are **challenges**. Challenges are trends, where all users can join and record a video while facing the challenge. Challenges are often a combination of three elements: text, sound, and movements. They can be started either by individuals, influencers or brands (Paul 2020b). For brands, challenges are an opportunity to start a viral trend and therefore, get a lot of attention to the brand or the company. For example, Guess started the branded hashtag challenge #InMyDenim and got over 5550 user-generated videos, 10.5 million video views, 14.3% engagement rate and over 12,000 additional followers for Guess' business account on TikTok (Docherty 2020).

The centerpiece of TikTok is the **"For You" page**. It is a feed of videos which are recommended to the user, based on their activity in the app. Users can choose to add a specific video to favorites or select "not interested" on videos on their "For you" page. It is also possible to follow specific influencers and content creators. If users follow a specific account, the videos of this accounts are shown on the "Following"

Fig. 6.1 TikTok US adult user distribution by age (Iqbal 2020b)

page. Moreover, videos can be easily shared with friends (TikTok 2020). The videos uploaded to TikTok cover a wide range of topics and content: from lip syncing to music, dancing, challenges and comedy to magic tricks (InfluencerMarketingHub 2020b, May 26). While everyone can upload videos to TikTok, over 50% of the users are below age 35 (Haoran 2020, Sloane and Rittenhouse 2019). In Fig. 6.1 the age distribution of TikTok users in the US is shown.

The TikTok Business Model

The mother company of TikTok is Byte Dance, a Chinese technology company. Byte Dance first launched Douyin for the Chinese market in September 2016 and later launched TikTok in 2017 for iOS and Android in most markets outside of China. Following the merger with Musical.ly on 2nd of August 2018 (Haoran 2020), TikTok became available in the US market. The merger of Musical.ly and TikTok was a strategic move of Byte Dance to unite all its users on a single platform (InfluencerMarketingHub 2020c, July 12). Today, TikTok is used in over 150 countries and is available in 75 languages all over the world. Given its Chinese roots, largest userbase of TikTok is in Asia (see Fig. 6.2), where over a third of internet users aged 16–64 have an account on the platform (Kavanagh 2019).

As COVID-19 pandemic emerged around the world in 2020, social media platforms such as TikTok were used for a variety of purposes: communicating with friends and family, information about the current status of corona infections and hygiene measures, and entertainment. Because the circumstances during COVID-19 pandemic strongly differed from the "normal" life, social media platforms have been used for different purposes than the ones they were actually designed for (Zheng et al. 2020). For example, the video communication platform Zoom is used as a platform for teachers to educate their students. Hence, social

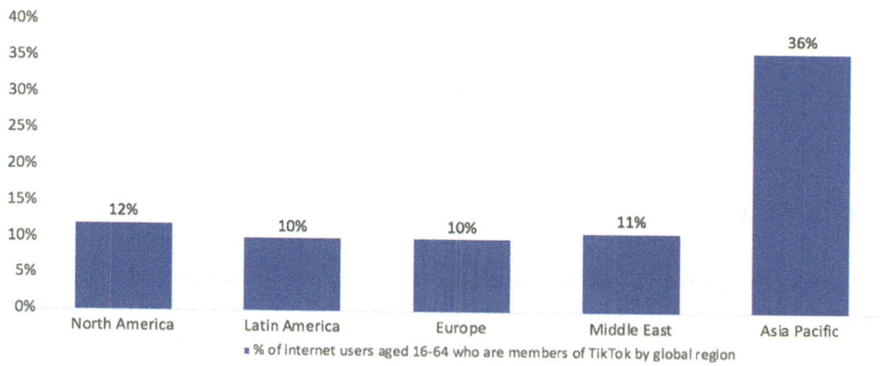

Fig. 6.2 Usages of TikTok around the world (Kavanagh 2019)

media platforms have to adapt to changing requirements in order to harness the potential benefits a global crisis can bring.

Analysis of the Literature

In order to answer the abovementioned research question, I reviewed the existing literature in relevant journals and on the internet from research and practice. Since this is a contemporary topic, the review is rather inclusive and has not been restricted to specific journals or rankings. As a result, I conducted a three-step process in order to develop the following three research deliverables:

1. A theoretical overview on social media platforms using the example of TikTok.
2. A trajectory of the evolution due to COVID-19 of TikTok.
3. An outlook toward the evolution of TikTok after COVID-19.

First, the current research literature on social media platforms and TikTok as well as the literature on COVID-19 implications toward social media platforms with special interest on TikTok were identified by conducting a review of the literature. The literature review has been conducted using relevant databases with appropriate keywords: "COVID-19", "digital technologies", "change", "TikTok", as well as "social media". Also, synonyms and modifications of these keywords have been included in the search.

Second, relevant articles have been identified through a forward and backward search. The forward search has been implemented by means of LitSonar (Sturm and Sunyaev 2019) and a manual search of selected databases that are not available in LitSonar. Following the identification of articles using the forward search, I reviewed the references of articles that matched the studies objectives, increasing our search scope.

Third, publications on customer behavior of digital technologies with a focus on TikTok were searched. The respective articles and authors were checked for credibility before including them in our review.

Findings from the Review

Following the review of the literature, I present four key findings on the evolution and success of TikTok during the COVID-19 pandemic. First, I discuss the properties that made TikTok so successful during the pandemic. Second, I summarize TikTok's role as marketing platform. Third, I provide an overview of TikTok as a learning platform during the pandemic. Fourth, I review threats to the future success of TikTok.

TikTok Success Factors

Overall, TikTok experienced a strong increase in the number of downloads. I distilled three main properties of TikTok that favored its success during the COVID-19 pandemic (see Table 6.1):

(i) TikTok's hyper-personalized algorithm,
(ii) TikTok as anti-social media platform, and
(iii) increased use of TikTok by influencers during corona pandemic.

I discuss each property in depth.

Table 6.1 Summary of findings

Findings	Description
Success factors	Three key properties catalyzed the recent success of TikTok: Hyper-personalized algorithm based on artificial intelligence, Anti-social approach—everybody can use the platform without registration, and Influencers migration lead to more content and more users
Marketing platform	TikTok seeks to establish itself as a marketing platform by Being a marketing partner, offering different ways of marketing products and brands and Collaborating with companies to help people in times of crisis
Learning platform	TikTok invests into the creation of educational content using the hashtag #LearnOnTikTok and called charities, universities and professionals to create educational content on TikTok
Future threats	Political leaders have raised concerns about the company related to privacy, security, and politics and discussed possible bans of the platform Aggressive competitors copy TikTok's functionality in order to provide features on their own platform or to launch a competing product

First, the main success factor of TikTok is the **hyper-personalized algorithm** based on artificial intelligence. The user receives video recommendations based on their individual view history, rewatches, likes, comments, shares and post-view activities (Hutchinson 2020b). The algorithm recommends only content that fits the profile. Thus, users have no effort searching for influencers or content that fits their interests. Especially, in times of the COVID-19 pandemic, this promises easy access to entertainment that users are craving for as a pastime while staying at home. Statistics show that the average time users spend on TikTok on a daily basis is higher than on any other platforms (Verto Analytics 2019). Since users see more and more videos with endless scrolling, the time spend on TikTok is hard to track and users are easily constantly provided with new content, because with every swipe a newly recommended video starts automatically. TikTok does not show the top bar of the phone, providing users with more screen size for the platform's content and removing possible distractions that could discontinue the platform's use. Therefore, the users have no indicator of how much time they already spent on TikTok.

Second, TikTok is the largest social-media platform following an **anti-social approach** (Novak 2020). To use TikTok, neither friends nor followers are needed. It is even possible to use the platform, watch videos and get personal recommendations without an account. Only when a user wants to upload videos, to follow video creators and to comment of content an account is needed (TikTok 2020). Since the "For You" page videos are recommended to users, it is not important to have many followers. Followers are more likely to get videos recommended from accounts they like. However, in principle, every video can be shown on the "For you" page and therefore, every video creator has the chance to be recognized by a large number of users (Novak 2020). TikTok is not build upon the principle of community building like other social media platforms, but on the principle of offering a platform for sharing creative videos for everybody (TikTok 2020). Therefore, its users have a platform to be recognized and express themselves even in times of COVID-19.

Third, the download rate of TikTok spiked during the COVID-19 pandemic as more and more **influencers** created accounts and content on TikTok. These influencers already had a huge fanbase on other Social Media Platforms. By creating TikTok content they brought their fans onto this platform. This resulted not only in an increasing number of users, but also exposed TikTok to an older generation. From February to March 2020, the number of influencers sharing videos throughout TikTok increased by 65% (Schwär 2020). This begs the question of why influencers opted for TikTok rather than any other platform. TikTok offers additional reach and marketing opportunities, but also an additional narrative level. It allows influencers to entertain their fans beyond their normal Social Media content. A fashion-influencer known for his perfect photos on Instagram, can also show less perfect videos of himself on TikTok. For example, uploading a video with double chin or a fail video that give him a human touch, making him more reachable for his fans (Schwär 2020). Especially, during COVID-19 pandemic, influencers had no chance to meet fans on fairs and events. Thus, they needed a new way to have social interactions.

These three **properties supported the growth** of TikTok during corona pandemic, TikTok now has more opportunities to diversify the platform and attract even more users. While TikTok was mainly a short-video sharing platform for entertainment, there are two main purposes resulting from the COVID-19 pandemic that allow TikTok to increase its userbase: as a marketing platform and as a learning platform.

TikTok as a Marketing Platform

Through the wide range of users, TikTok is becoming an attractive platform for brands and businesses to advertise their products and even themselves as a valuable employer. Since TikTok is a relatively young platform, there is no universal formula for successful marketing on TikTok. However, TikTok allows businesses to advertise their products and themselves in creative ways (TikTok 2020).

So far, TikTok is unmonetized but some comments highlight the potential threat for other online ad players, if TikTok rolls out a broader ad product (Krause 2020). Especially the integration of Sprinklr with TikTok brings new marketing power to its customers. Sprinklr is a leading customer experience management platform (Sprinklr 2020). The integration of Sprinklr enables in-feed video ads and therefore a new way of advertising on the platform for businesses. The ads are played as autoplay and sound-on version in full-screen within the "For You"-Page (Lewanczik 2020). In general, there are three ways of advertising on TikTok for businesses (InfluencerMarketingHub 2020a; Sbai 2020): (1) In-feed native ads: Bidding for spots for ads to serve them to targeted users. (2) Brand takeover ads: Ad will be played at targeted TikTok users while opening the app. (3) Hashtag challenges: Invite users to imitate and offer the opportunity of UGC (Sbai 2020). Each business has to evaluate which of these three ways–or perhaps a combination of them is the most promising marketing approach that suits their needs.

In April 2020, together with business partners TikTok launched "Small Gestures", another new marketing initiative. The initiative seeks to connect the community while maintaining social distance. The basic idea is to "give back and spark joy throughout the TikTok community" (Newsroom TikTok 2020). Through the collaboration with the brand partners, TikTok is able to give users the opportunity to send gifts to someone who might be in need. The "Small Gestures" are offered for free from the brand partners for all TikTok users, who can send up to three gifts (SmartInsights 2020). The initiative shows that TikTok wants to further expand their position as marketing partner for businesses.

TikTok as a Learning Platform

Besides TikTok's strive to become a platform for businesses to advertise their brands and products, TikTok also wants to establish itself as a learning platform. It supports the upload of learning content, for example, in the form of videos. With the program #LearnOnTikTok, TikTok launched a program in May 2020 in order to help facilitate learning during lockdown. The hashtag #LearnOnTikTok already has more than seven billion views and over one million videos (Joseph 2020), suggesting its success.

TikTok has "announced plans to commission hundreds of experts and institutions to produce educational content for the platform" (Iqbal 2020a). Therefore, TikTok wants to pay universities and charities to create educational content and experts in a specific field to produce professional videos (Paul 2020a). For example, at the initiative's launch, TikTok included videos with the British actor Sean Sagar sharing tips on preparing for auditions and the TV presenter and mathematician Rachel Riley helping to develop math skills (Iqbal 2020a). The goal is to establish hundreds of educators, real-world skills creators, and non-profit organizations creating educational content for the platform (TikTok 2020). In order to incentivize the content production, a $50 million fund has been offered for creative learning on the platform (Hutchinson 2020a).

Diversifying the content on the platform opens up new possibilities for more strategic content partnership, the opportunity for users to engage with brands, and for brands and businesses to create content that creates societal value, rather than purely economic value (Joseph 2020). Hence, the growth of the marketing platform and the learning platform are closely related.

Threats to the Future Success of TikTok

Due to the increasing number of users, TikTok poses a threat to competitors and political leaders have raised privacy, security, and political concerns about Byte Dance as a Chinese company. For example, the United States consider banning all Chinese social media platforms including TikTok for national security concerns (Pham 2020). Even though no decision has been made, the threat is quite severe. A ban of the platform in the United States would mean losing about 165 million users for TikTok (Mohsin 2020). While the United States are still discussing a ban of the platform, India already took actions. India banned nearly 60 Chinese apps including TikTok (Pham 2020). The platform had about 200 million users from India before it was blocked (Singh 2020).

Banning TikTok makes room for competitors to take over the market. While direct competitors such as Facebook Inc. tried to cover the functions of TikTok on their own platforms, the company also tried launching a TikTok-like platform under the name Lasso back in 2019. Since the benefits did not materialize, it was shut down on July 10th 2020 (Porter 2020). Facebook Inc. already invested in the development of the predecessor of Lasso, Instagram Reels. After a testing phase in Brazil, Instagram Reels was launched in France and Germany on 24th June 2020 (ibid).

Against this background, the current popularity of TikTok does not guarantee its continuous success in order to reach popularity levels of Instagram and Facebook. Other platforms have been at this juncture before. For example, vine was an extremely popular video-sharing platform back in the days, yet nowadays they disappeared (InfluencerMarketingHub 2020b, May 26). The above-mentioned threats force TikTok to diversify its portfolio in order to sustain competition. The approach to capitalize on brand engagements and expanding their social media marketing reach has been suggested as a positive indicator for its ongoing success (InfluencerMarketingHub 2020b, May 26; Novak 2020). In a similar vein, the platform's anti-social approach could have more staying power than traditional models of social media platforms "that suffer from context collapse, where the value of the product eventually goes down as a user adds too many friends" (Novak 2020).

However, the continuous evolution of TikTok will be exciting, as TikTok did not take away usage from other social media platforms yet (Krause 2020). All social media platforms increased their usage rates during COVID-19. Therefore, social media platforms including TikTok have to show if they can hold the users and influencers when COVID-19 pandemic flattens, and users have less time to spend online.

Conclusion

All social media platforms experienced an increasing download and usage rate during COVID-19 pandemic (Krause 2020). Due to its increased userbase, TikTok is now able to diversify the platform and position itself to fight the competition on its way to establishing itself as the biggest social media platform. This chapter gave an overview about the evolution of TikTok during COVID-19 and a first outlook on how the platform can evolve in the future. Since there is limited research on TikTok and the impact of COVID-19, there are several points future research can investigate:

1. Further explore and explain successful marketing on TikTok
2. Investigate the consequences of TikTok's ban in certain countries. What does this mean for TikTok and how do users react to such a ban?
3. Further research could explore how the function of Instagram Reels can fully map all functions of TikTok and TikTok's response to such competitive actions.
4. Further investigation is needed on the decreased usage of TikTok, or in general on social media platforms, as a result of decreasing quarantine measures.

Moving forward, TikTok focuses on its role as a marketing tool and the expansion of content creators on the platform through collaborations. The goals are to become an indispensable partner for businesses and to offer a bigger variety of content while expanding the target group. Furthermore, the restrictions of countries against TikTok and the concerns raised by political leaders threaten TikTok's position in the global market. The success story of TikTok started before COVID-19 and was supported due to the quarantine measures during the global pandemic. Many people look with great excitement toward the future evolution of TikTok and whether it can establish itself in the long run.

References

Aerzteblatt. (2020). *COVID-19: Die Hashtags der Krise*. Retrieved June 25, 2020, from https://www.aerzteblatt.de/nachrichten/111302/COVID-19-Die-Hashtags-der-Krise

Carr, C., & Hayes, R. (2015). Social media: Defining, developing, and divining. *Atlantic Journal of Communication, 23*(1), 46–65. https://doi.org/10.1080/15456870.2015.972282.

Clement, J. (2020a). *Leading Android apps worldwide 2020, by downloads*. Retrieved July 1, 2020, from https://www.statista.com/statistics/693944/leading-android-apps-worldwide-by downloads/

Clement, J. (2020b). *Leading iPhone apps worldwide 2020, by downloads*. Retrieved July 1, 2020, from https://www.statista.com/statistics/695791/top-iphone-apps-worldwide-by-number-of downloads/

Cullinan, E. (2020). *Why we lack motivation to work during a global pandemic*. Retrieved July 1, 2020, from https://www.welcometothejungle.com/en/articles/lack-motivation-during-corona-crisis

Daugherty, T., Eastin, M., & Bright, L. (2008). Exploring consumer motivations for creating user-generated content. *Journal of Interactive Advertising, 8*(2), 16–25. https://doi.org/10.1080/15252019.2008.10722139.

Docherty, K. (2020). 12 *TikTok challenges to inspire your next campaign*. Retrieved July 1, 2020, from https://later.com/blog/tiktok-challenges/

Hallikainen, P. (2015). Why people use social media platforms: Exploring the motivations and consequences of use. In L. Mola, F. Pennarola, & S. Za (Eds.), *From information to smart society*. Lecture Notes in Information Systems and Organisation (Vol. 5). Cham: Springer.

Haoran. (2020). *TikTok: Using AI to take over the world*. Retrieved July 1, 2020, from https://digital.hbs.edu/platform-digit/submission/tik-tok-using-ai-to-take-over-the world/

Hutchinson, A. (2020a, May 28). *TikTok announces #LearnOnTikTok initiative to encourage education during lockdowns*. Retrieved July 7, 2020, from https://www.socialmediatoday.com/news/tiktok-announces-learnontiktok-initiative-to-encourage-education-during-lo/578805/

Hutchinson, A. (2020b, June 18). *How TikTok's algorithm works – as explained by TikTok*. Retrieved July 1, 2020, from https://www.socialmediatoday.com/news/how-tiktoks-algorithm-works-as-explained-by-tiktok/580153/

InfluencerMarketingHub. (2020a, January 2). *How much do TikTok Ads cost?* Retrieved July 1, 2020, from https://influencermarketinghub.com/how-much-do-tiktok-ads-cost/)

InfluencerMarketingHub. (2020b, May 26). *What is TikTok? What you need to know about the new Musical.ly*. Retrieved from https://influencermarketinghub.com/what-is-tiktok/

InfluencerMarketingHub. (2020c, July 12). *TikTok-Marketing für Anfänger – Ein Marketing-Handbuch für Werbung auf TikTok*. Retrieved July 1, 2020, from https://influencermarketinghub.com/de/tiktok-marketing-anfaenger/

Iqbal, O. (2020a). *TikTok makes moves into education market*. Retrieved July 10, 2020, from https://www.bbc.com/news/technology-53079625

Iqbal W. (2020b). *TikTok revenue and usage statistics*. Retrieved July 10, 2020, from https://www.businessofapps.com/data/tik-tok-statistics/

Johnson, J. (2020a). *Online media use changes during the coronavirus pandemic in Europe 2020*. Retrieved July 1, 2020, from https://www.statista.com/statistics/1110864/online-media-use-during-the-coronavirus-pandemic-europe/

Johnson, T. (2020b). *The rise of TikTok during COVID-19*. Retrieved June 25, 2020, from https://tinuiti.com/blog/marketing-news-covid-19/tiktok-covid-19/

Joseph, S. (2020). *'A shift towards maturity': Why TikTok is investing $15m in short-form educational content in Europe*. Retrieved July 10, 2020, from https://digiday.com/media/a-shift-towards-maturity-why-tiktok-is-investing-15m-in-short-form-educational-content-in-europe/

Kaplan, A., & Haenlein, M. (2010). Users of the world, unite! The challenges and opportunities of social media. *Business Horizons, 53*(1), 59–68. https://doi.org/10.1016/j.bushor.2009.09.003.

Kavanagh, D. (2019). Is time against TikTok? Retrieved from https://blog.globalwebindex.com/chart-of-the-week/time-against-tiktok/

Krause, R. (2020, May 18). TikTok raises profile in digital ads, hires Disney streaming boss as CEO. *Investor's Business Daily*. Retrieved from https://search.proquest.com/docview/2404160634?accountid=10218

Lewanczik, N. (2020). *TikTok: Neue features und API Öffnung liefern mehr Optionen für TikToker und Advertiser*. Retrieved July 7, 2020, from https://onlinemarketing.de/news/tiktok-neue-features-api-oeffnung-optionen-tiktoker

LLC. (2020, April 25). Tik tok's challenge that binds families during coronavirus quarantine. *CE Noticias Financieras*. Retrieved July 1, 2020, from https://search.proquest.com/docview/2394770938?accountid=10218

Maslow, A. H. (1943). A theory of human motivation. *Psychological Review, 50*, 370–396. Retrieved from http://citeseerx.ist.psu.edu/viewdoc/download?doi=10.1.1.318.2317&rep=rep1&type=pdf

Mohsin, M. (2020). *10 TikTok statistics that you need to know in 2020 [Infographics]*. Retrieved July 7, 2020, from https://www.oberlo.com/blog/tiktok-statistics

Newsroom TikTok. (2020). *TikTok small gestures launches with brand partners to give back*. Retrieved July 7, 2020, from https://newsroom.tiktok.com/de-de/tiktok-small-gestures-launches with-brand-partners-to-give-back

Nikolinakou, A., & Phua, J. (2019). Do human values matter for promoting brands on social media? How social media users' values influence valuable brand-related activities such as sharing, content creation, and reviews. *Journal of Consumer Behaviour, 19*(1), 13–23. https://doi.org/10.1002/cb.1790.

Novak, T. (2020). *The rise of TikTok and understanding its parent company, ByteDance*. Retrieved July 1, 2020, from https://turner.substack.com/p/the-rise-of-tiktok-and-understanding

Obar, J. A., & Wildman, S. (2015). Social media definition and the governance challenge: An introduction to the special issue. *Telecommunications Policy, 39*(9), 745–750.

Paul, K. (2020a). *It's corona time': TikTok helpy teens cope with the coronavirus pandemic*. Retrieved June 25, 2020, from https://www.theguardian.com/world/2020/mar/12/coronavirus-outbreak-tik-tok-memes

Paul, M. (2020b). *How to use TikTok challenges for business*. Retrieved July 7, 2020, from https://www.socialmediaexaminer.com/how-to-use-tiktok-challenges-for-business/

Pham, S. (2020). *TikTok ban undercuts ByteDance in one of the world's biggest digital markets*. Retrieved July 13, 2020, from https://edition.cnn.com/2020/06/30/tech/tiktok-india-ban-intl-hnk/index.html

Porter, J. (2020). *Facebook's TikTok clone Lasso will shut down this month*. Retrieved July 13, 2020, from https://www.theverge.com/2020/7/2/21311077/facebook-lasso-shutting-down-tiktok short-form-video-hobbi

Sbai, A. (2020). *Hashtag Challenges als Trend: TikTok auf dem Vormarsch*. Retrieved July 11, 2020, from https://onlinemarketing.de/news/hashtag-challenges-tiktok-vormarsch

Schwär, H. (2020). *TikTok bricht sämtliche Download-Rekorde – dank Langeweile in der Isolation*. Retrieved July 5, 2020, from https://www.gruenderszene.de/media/tiktok-download-rekord-corona?interstitial

Shao, G. (2009). Understanding the appeal of user-generated media: A uses and gratification perspective. *Internet Research, 19*(1), 7–25. https://doi.org/10.1108/10662240910927795.

Singh, M. (2020). *TikTok goes down in India, its biggest overseas market*. Retrieved July 13, 2020, from https://techcrunch.com/2020/06/30/tiktok-goes-down-in-india-its-biggest-overseas-market

Sloane, G., & Rittenhouse, L. (2019). First look at TikTok's game plan: Leaked pitch deck reveals how the app is luring brands. Spoiler alert: There will be gummy bears. *Advertising Age, 90*(20), 6. Retrieved from https://search.proquest.com/docview/2306286732?rfr_id=info%3Axri%2Fsid%3Aprimo

SmartInsights. (2020). *TikTok – Launches 'Small Gestures' on its social media platform*. Retrieved July 15, 2020, from https://www.smartinsights.com/social-media-marketing/social-media-strategy/tiktok small-gestures-virtual-gift-giving-social-media-platform/

Sprinklr. (2020). Retrieved July 15, 2020, from https://www.sprinklr.com/de/

Sturm, B., & Sunyaev, A. (2019). Design principles for systematic search systems: A holistic synthesis of a rigorous multicycle design science research journey. *Business & Information Systems Engineering, 61*(1), 91–111.

TikTok. (2020). Retrieved from https://www.tiktok.com

Verto Analytics. (2019, November 12). Most popular mobile social networking apps in the United States as of September 2019, by average session duration (in minutes) [Graph]. *Statista*. Retrieved July 15, 2020, from https://www.statista.com/statistics/579411/top-us-socialnetworking-apps-ranked-by-session-length/

Werder, K., Helms, R.W., & Jansen, S. (2014). Social media for success: A strategic framework. In *Pacific Asia conference on information systems 2014*, AISeL, Chengdu, PRC, Paper 92.

Xu, L., Yan, X., & Zhang, Z. (2019). Research on the causes of the "TikTok" app becoming popular and the existing problems. *Journal of Advanced Management Science, 7*(2). Retrieved from http://www.joams.com/uploadfile/2019/0613/20190613034911476.pdf

Zheng, T., Foschi, L., Haynie, M., Lyster, L., Pittard. B., Dirkx, D., Low, B., Friedman, K., & Kelly, S., (2020). *The role of social media during the coronavirus pandemic*. Retrieved July 10, 2020, from https://www.pmg.com/blog/the-role-of-social-media-during-the-coronavirus pandemic/?cn-reloaded=1

Chapter 7
How Can Software Development Teams Be Controlled During the COVID-19 Pandemic

Zacharias Schrage

Abstract The COVID-19 pandemic forced companies to rethink how and where the employees work as well as how to control them. This lead to an increased reliance on digital services. Drawing on the literature of control theory, this chapter presents a literature review using on control practices that have been used to control agile and/or traditional software development teams, that is, the teams that develop the very same services everyone now relies upon. Based on a review of 25 journal articles, I develop possible adaptions to remote environments for the identified control practices. 60 control practices are identified for agile software development, whereas 36 control practices are identified for traditional software development teams. Many control practices identified, especially those associated with formal or self-control, can be enacted during the pandemic without adaption. While some control practices need to be adapted, others—mostly those associated with clan control—can be emulated via digital services although the effectiveness is questionable.

Keywords Agile software development · Control practices · COVID-19 · Formal control · Informal control · Software development · Working remotely

Introduction

The COVID-19 pandemic is omnipresent by now and affects everyone, including schools, universities, and businesses. Due to social distancing guidelines in order to slow down the spread of the virus, organizations have been confronted with new challenges. For example, schools and universities have started to use video conference service to hold classes and lectures. Businesses have moved their employees into remote and home office work, where possible. One consequence has been the decentralization of a workforce that used to share the same office space.

Z. Schrage (✉)
University of Cologne, Cologne, Germany

C. Hovestadt et al. (eds.), *Digital Responses to Covid-19*, SpringerBriefs in Information Systems, https://doi.org/10.1007/978-3-030-66611-8_7

Consequently, employees have limited means of interaction with each other as well as their middle and top management. From a management perspective, this suggests a lack of control over the employees. This is a problem as management still needs to ensure that projects are on track and will meet customers' needs (Kirsch 1996, p. 1). From an operational perspective, remote work presents new challenges in work modes that are built around frequent interaction, shared spaces and co-location. Software development is one such area of work.

Organizations adopting social distancing guidelines switched many routines and business practices from the physical space to the digital realm (Yoo et al. 2012, p. 1400). As such, organizations increase rely on digitally enabled service offerings to maintain their business operations. Examples include, video conferencing tools, e-commerce solutions, and workflow tools. Hence, organizations increasingly rely on software technologies to run their business operations, increasing demands for software developers. Software development teams need to deliver the best possible product while aligning team goals with the organization's business goals (Kirsch 1996, p. 1). However, software development organizations face the same pandemic constraints. They cannot physically interact with their customers, nor can their developers be co-located.

The increasing demands for software development organization in conjunction with the constraints of the COVID-19 pandemic raise new challenges toward controls enforced by management. In this situation, many things are in flux and unclear, such as which control instruments management can and cannot use, and whether or not these instruments require adaptation. Hence, this chapter seeks to answer the following research questions:

> How does the COVID-19 Pandemic affect how software development teams can be controlled?

The remainder of this chapter is structured as follows. First we give an overview of the literature on control modes and software development methods, followed by a description of the applied research method. Within the analysis and results, control practices are identified and a method is proposed. The method helps to enact and adapt practices that cannot be enacted in their normal way. To close of the paper the results and possible direction for future research are discussed.

Control Modes

Overall, we distinguish between formal and informal control modes. Control modes try to align the goals of the controllees with the goals of the controller. The term formal control mode alludes to the fact that the controller enacts the written down controls in a top-down manner (Jaworski 1988, p. 26). Informal control mode on the other hand "are unwritten, typically worker-initiated mechanisms that influence the behavior of individuals or groups" (Jaworski 1988, p. 26). The choice of formal control mode and informal control mode does not have to be an either-or choice, but rather an ambidextrous view about the best symbioses of the two (Gregory and Keil

2014, p. 352). The ambidextrous use of control modes is often implemented using control portfolios, that is, “a mix of overlapping and redundant mechanisms used to exercise these modes of control” (Kirsch 1997, p. 215).

Formal Control Modes

The literature differentiates between different formal control modes based on the time at which the controller enacts the controls (Jaworski 1988, p. 26): Input control (e.g., Wiener et al. 2016, p. 743), behavior control (Jaworski 1988, p. 26), and outcome control (Wiener et al. 2016, p. 743). In the following, we describe each mode in depth:

Behavior control is defined by the use of rules and processes in order to specify how to achieve a desired result. A reward structure promotes the adherence to the rules and processes. To use This control modes requires the controllee to be observable or the controller must have knowledge of the appropriate behavior (Kirsch 1997, p. 217). **Input control** describes the use of resource allocation and human resource practices to create teams, which are able to complete their assigned tasks. Therefore input control has to be enacted at the start of a project (Jaworski 1988, p. 26). As a formal control mode the rewards are given to “the controllee based on her ability to utilize allocated resources” (Wiener et al. 2016, p. 744).

Outcome control describes the use of predefined goals between the controlling and the controlled party. The attainment of these goals is measured and rewards or penalties are distributed based on how well the goals where reached irrespective of the controllee’s behavior or the process used to reach the goal (Kirsch 1996, p. 2). Outcome control with the final product as the goal may suggest only one point in time when the product is compared to the specified goals. However, outcome control can also be applied to interim products—sometimes referred to as emergent outcome control (Harris et al. 2009, p. 404)—allowing for changes or corrective actions. Consequently, stakeholders can steer the development towards a final result that satisfies their requirements (Harris et al. 2009, p. 404).

In sum, the goals can either be the final product or an intermediate result in the process to create the final product. When trying to align the controllees’ goals with the controller’s goals using formal control modes, the controller would use positive or negative incentives (Tiwana 2008, pp. 770–771). Positive incentives might be bonuses (e.g., for finishing projects within time, budget and quality). Negative incentives might be penalties (e.g., for not finishing in time, within budget or with sufficient quality).

Informal Control Modes

An alternative to formal controls are informal controls, that is, the controller has to align the controllees goals using “unwritten, typically worker-initiated mechanisms that influence the behavior of individuals or group" (Jaworski 1988, p. 26). Two control modes are classified as informal control mode: clan control and self-control.

Clan control refers to the influence of group or clan values and norms by the controller to align them with the project. Clan control describes an indirect effect, as the controllees are not influence by the controller directly, but rather by the values and norms of the group (Chua et al. 2012, p. 594). Hence, clan control requires agreed upon values, beliefs and norms among group members that work towards a common goal (Ouchi 1979, p. 838). The clan has to make sure that their members internalize the clan's beliefs, norms, and values and also spread these values (Ouchi 1979, p. 844). This is due to the informal and sometimes unwritten nature of these beliefs, norms, and values (Ouchi 1980, p. 137). Unlike in formal control modes, the clan does the monitoring the adherence of the clans values, belief and norms, nor does the clan sanction non-adhering members (Kirsch 1997, pp. 217–218).

Self-control is the second informal control mode, describing "performance evaluation schemes that reward autonomy and self-management" (Kirsch et al. 2002, p. 486). The principle behind self-control is: group members enacting self-control are able to (1) decide about next step that needs to be taken and (2) take the steps while adhering to the quality standards set by themselves. All of this is done without any outside influence (Henderson and Lee 1992, p. 760). As self-control is inherently self-motivated, the controllee and the controller are the same person. The monitoring, sanctioning and rewarding is therefore done by oneself (Kirsch 1996, p. 3).

Software Development Methods

Software development methods can be split into two categories. First, traditional software development methods that rely on a sequential process. Second, agile software development methods that rely on the principles of the "Agile Manifesto" by Beck et al. (2001).

Traditional software development methods (e.g., the waterfall model; see (Nerur et al. 2005, p. 74)) require the definition of all system requirements and architectural design components before the actual development and implementation process begins. While this simplifies the transition between requirements analysis and solution design, it creates many challenges during implementation. For example, variations in the process are viewed as undesirables, yet in today's fast changing environment requirements change naturally and frequently. Life cycle models guide the development by formalizing team members assigned roles, defining tasks and expected results. However, they are often rigid and the customer is mainly involved only in the planning process in order to define the requirements. Thereafter, the customer's participation is neither expected nor required (Nerur et al. 2005, pp. 74–75).

In response to these problems, the "Agile Manifesto" was developed around the year 2000 as an alternative approach to traditional software development methods (Highsmith 2001). Agile software development approaches (e.g., Scrum and

Extreme Programming (Highsmith 2001)) implement a variety of agile principles that the "Agile Manifesto" suggests. For example: people and interactions are more important than tools or processes. This led to the fundamental principle of co-location, where agile development teams are often co-located in order to ease and simplify the personal knowledge exchange and interaction (Teasley et al. 2002, pp. 680–681). Furthermore, the manifesto presents the idea that "[w]orking software is the primary measure of progress" (Beck et al. 2001), rather than documentation. A close collaborative relationship with the customer is viewed as more important than extensive contract negotiation. More so, changing customer requirements are welcomed even during later development stages (Beck et al. 2001). As such, agile software development has much in common with processes from the design space (Brhel et al. 2015, pp. 171–172).

Analysis

To understand how software development has changed during the COVID-19 pandemic and how such work could be controlled under the different circumstances, a systemic literature review is used, following prior guidelines (Webster and Watson 2002; Levy and Ellis 2006). In order to answer the research question, I review will analyze papers that study control modes and the control instruments. As such, this study includes articles on software development in remote teams as well as on co-located teams. Studies in the context of COVID-19 are of particular interest, as these may shed light the adaptation of control during the global pandemic.

Literature Sampling

First, the literature search is done by a keyword search for the terms control modes, information systems development or agile software development as well as their variations and synonyms. The categories title, keywords and abstract were searched with these keywords. The identified articles abstracts were screened to ensure relevancy for the purposes of this article. Following this keyword search, further articles were identified with a backwards and forward search (Levy and Ellis 2006, pp. 190–192). The same screening process was applied for the backwards and forward search as was for the keyword search.

The initial keyword search was limited to papers published in the journals or conferences ranked in the VHB-JOURQUAL 3 or listed by Levy and Ellis (2006). For those journals or conference proceedings only listed by Levy and Ellis (2006) the impact rating of the magazine needs to be higher than 1.0 at the time the article was published to ensure high quality and scientific relevance. The identified articles were then analyzed via a concept matrix (Webster and Watson 2002, pp. 16–17). The categories of the concept matrix are explained in the analysis section.

Literature Collection

The concept matrix consisted of four categories and was used to collect the data from the identified 25 articles. The four categories in the concept matrix are: research method, control modes, control practices, and software development methods. First, the research method of the analyzed papers were extracted. All papers are case studies or surveys with one exception of a literature review (i.e., Dreesen and Schmid 2018). Second, software development methods investigated in the paper were extracted. Third, the investigated control modes of each paper were extracted. Fourth, the control practices found in the studies were extracted. Only control practices that are part of behavior control and outcome control were analyzed, since input controls had to be implemented before the start of the project and hence cannot be influenced by a controller. Given that a single control practices can be used to enact multiple different control modes of both formal and informal nature, I do not differentiate between, which control practices can be used to enact which control modes.

Literature Analysis

The study identified 25 journal articles that were analyzed. We find the following *research methods*: 14 (56.0%) surveys, ten articles (40.0%) case studies and one literature review (4.0%). When analyzing for the *development method*, I find that nine (36.0%) articles studied agile software development projects, while five (20.0%) papers study traditional software development projects, and three (12.0%) articles study both agile and traditional teams. For eight articles (32.0%) the development methodologies could not be identified.

Since articles often study multiple *control modes*, our descriptive results of the analysis of control modes add up to more than 25 articles. In our primary dataset, only one article investigated only a single control mode. Outcome control was studied in 21 (84.0%) of the 25 papers, of which one (4.0%) explicitly studied emergent outcome control. Behavior control was studied in 18 (72.0%) of the articles and another 18 (72.0%) of the articles studied clan control. Self-control was a topic of interest in 15 (60%) of the papers. For two (8.0%) papers it was not possible to identify the studied control modes. Huber et al. (2013) only differentiate between formal and informal control but not the associated control modes and for Conboy et al. (2011) the control modes could not be identify.

Within our primary dataset we find numerous *control practices* that enact control modes. Categorizing the papers by development method, I found 60 control practices in studies that investigate *agile software development*. However, list 29 of these control practices are listed in a review paper (Dreesen and Schmid 2018), whereas 31 are extracted from empirical studies. I find 34 control practices in papers that investigate *traditional software development*. Furthermore, I find 36 control practices in articles that did not clearly articulate their investigated development method. However, the results might be confounded through varying units of analysis in these articles. For example, Srivastava and Teo (2012) differentiate between self-governance, and self-goal-setting, self-reward, self-sanction (p. 123), while Keil et al. (2013) view self-goal setting, self-procedure setting and also autonomous setting of a time frame as part of self-management. Therefore, for the purposes of this paper all of them, are subsumed under the control practice of self-management. The same applies to the control practice of self-monitoring.

While comparison of control practices across methodologies found a good fit, we could not find a match for seven control practices. For three control practices, the standardization of performance criteria as well as the decentralization of either performance criteria or method (Nidumulo and Subramani 2003, pp. 165–167), the inability to find fitting control practices can be attributed to the specificity of the control practices. While it is possible to argue that for example self-management captures part of the decentralization of methods, it is still only a partial equivalency, while the standardization of methods can be viewed as the equivalent of predefined behaviors and procedures. In the case of the four control practices the lack of equivalents, which part of the control practices used in the paper by Choudhury and Sabherwal (2003) can in part be attributed to the use a case study to gain an in-depth view into the five cases studied and the control practices may be specific to certain problems.

Findings

The following section presents ideas on how the control practices identified from the in-depth analysis of the 25 journal articles on whether and how they can be used to control teams during the COVID-19 pandemic. Control practices in agile software development, for which adherence can be tested after the fact and therefore, can be used during the COVID-19 pandemic include predefined behavior, rules, and procedures (see Table 7.1).

Table 7.1 Overview of control practices for use during the COVID-19 pandemic

Category	Exemplary control practices for agile software development
Control practices can be used as is	Continuous integration, code reviews, collective ownership
Control practices require adaptations	Burndown charts, daily scrum, retrospective stand-up meetings, sprint planning meetings, storyboards, user stories
Control practices are not applicable, or their effects are unclear	Coaching, on-site developers, socialization, sprint review meeting, sustainable pace, team co-location, training meetings, workshops

Adapting Control Practices from Agile Software Development

One example of a control practice in agile software development are coding standards. The enactment of coding standards does not require close proximity between controller and controllee, but rather the exchange of the source code that can be shared via version control systems like Git (Software Freedom Conservancy). The adherence can be determined by inspecting the code afterwards. For agile teams, the control practices of collective ownership, continuous integration and code reviews also require access to the source code to be enacted (Agile Alliance). The use of version control systems can be considered a requirement for any software development teams operating during the COVID-19 pandemic, regardless of its applied method. Practice guides and training brochures can also be enabled digitally by distributing them in a digital format rather than printed.

Meetings with a formal nature, like sprint planning meetings, as well as meetings of the informal kind can be adapted to be done via video conference services rather than in person. The control practice of the planning game can be done during the pandemic with the help of video conference services or voice over IP services due to the simple process used for estimation (Agile Alliance). Other examples of meetings, that can be done via video conference services are the daily scrum or retrospective stand-up meetings as these meetings only require basic video conferencing functionalities to be enacted (Agile Alliance). As such, the use of messenger services like Slack is not affected by the COVID-19 pandemic just like the use of unit testing or the use of acceptance tests. Agile control practices like user stories, to organize and split the project into individual function parts (Agile Alliance), storyboards or burndown charts, which are used to "track the amount of output [. . .] a team has completed across an iteration or a project" (Agile Alliance) can be done digitally using online services such as Azure Dev Ops (Microsoft 2019). Pair programming can be enacted remotely via digital services. One example service is Visual Studio Live Share (Microsoft).

While it may seem like all control practices using meetings can be held via video conference service, there are also exceptions like the sprint review meeting. The sprint review meeting is there to discuss and show the current working parts and implemented functionalities of the project to the stakeholders in an iteration demo as well as offering an avenue for feedback and change requests (Agile Alliance). Whether it is possible to conduct such a meeting via a video conference may depend on other factors such as project type and project stage. A web-based application is an example project type that can be presented and discussed online, whereas virtual reality project would be more difficult or impossible to present and discuss due to specialized hardware requirements. Other control practices that may face problems depend on the context. Workshops, coaching, and training meetings give rise to similar challenges as the sprint review meeting.

Video conferences are a very useful tool to enact many types of meetings. However, the transition from personal meetings to video conferences may be more difficult or even impossible for meetings that seek socialization. While it is possible to hold a book club meeting without significant changes using video conferencing services, other social activities like a joint team dinner are more difficult to realize. This may affect the relationship between team members and the team's rituals and ceremonies cannot be enacted. Rituals and ceremonies are important parts of a team (Ouchi 1979, p. 844) and their absence make it difficult to propagate and spread team values. Sitting together in an open workspace during implementation is no longer a feasible control practices, if the organization follows social distancing guidelines. A possible way to adapt these practices could be to emulate them by using video conferencing services: Although it is not known whether similar effects can be achieved, other agile control practices cannot be enacted at all, for example on-site developers or team co-location.

Another control practices, such as sustainable pace, simply cannot be enacted directly. Given the controllers is not able to check the working hours of the controlee, a workaround would have to be introduced, for example, talking to the controllee about the importance of work-life balance or logging of system use, whereas the latter comes with severe privacy concerns. Talking to the employee rather calls for the need of self-management. Self-management can be enacted during the COVID-19 pandemic and rather gains in importance. Given the lack or less severe motivations in a remote setup, self-management becomes an important motivational driver for employees. Otherwise prominent motivations, such as peer pressure or group recognition, have less effect with social distance.

However, reliance on the self-management practice of self-control can be a problem for agile development team. While low requirement changes in conjunction with high self-control leads to better development outcomes, high requirement changes and high self-control has negative implications. The software becomes more complex and bug severity increases (Maruping et al. 2009, p. 391). Table 7.2 provides an overview of the identified control practices with their suggested adaptation.

Control Practices from Traditional Software Development

Turning to the control practices used in traditional software development, a significant number of practices overlap with those uncovered earlier. For example, peer pressure is a control practice that agile software development teams also use (Kirsch 1997; Persson et al. 2012). Examples equivalents in traditional software development would be feedback from team member (Henderson and Lee 1992, p. 760) and group recognition and dialogue (Persson et al. 2012, p. 415).

We find three unique control practices that do not have an equivalent. These are the top down work assignments (Henderson and Lee 1992, p. 763), the "inspection of documentation and reports" (Gregory et al. 2013, p. 1221) "and "intercultural" workshops to foster shared understanding about mutual social practices" (Gregory et al. 2013, p. 1219). The reason for the non-existence of an equivalent control practices roots in the agile manifest. In an agile team certain degree of specialization

Table 7.2 Overview of control practices and possible adaptations for use in remote agile software development

Control mode	Control practices for agile software development	Possible adaptations
Behavior control	Code reviews	Remote enactment by using version control systems like Git to share code
	Coding standards	Remote enactment by using version control systems like Git to share code and by checking adherence after each commit (possible option for automation)
	Continuous integration	Remote enactment by using version control systems like Git to share code
	Daily scrum	Remote enactment by using video conference services, timers, and digital services for progress tracking
	Open workspace	Emulation by using video conference services, though whether an effect similar to the on-site enactment can be achieved is questionable
	Pair programming	Enactment by using specialized digital services, for example, visual studio live share
	Practice guides	Distribution in digital formats, benefitting from the mutability of digital media for continuous updates
	Training brochures	Distribution in digital format or adaption to different formats such as training videos
	Training meetings	Pre-recording training videos and offering Q&A sessions using video conference services
Clan control	Book clubs	Remote enactment by using video conference services
	Collective ownership	Remote enactment by using version control systems like Git to share code
	Group recognition	Enhancing the retrospective meeting with an additional component to highlight excellent work of certain team members
	Informal meetings	Using video conference services or text messaging services such as WhatsApp or slack
	Peer pressure	Remote enactment via positive reinforcement during meetings, for example, praising team members, who worked long hours or committed significant amounts of code
	Planning game	Voice over IP services and online services for planning poker or using video conference services and actual cards by team members
	Retrospective stand-up meetings	Using video conference services and timers to ensure the meeting does not exceed its limits due to sitting team members
	Socialization (e.g. joint team dinner)	Remote enactment by using video conference services, though effectiveness and feasibility are questionable
Outcome control	Burndown charts	Remote enactment by using online service, such as Azure
	Sprint planning meeting	Using video conference services and online services to track the development progress such as Azure DevOps
	Sprint review meeting—iteration demo	Adaption depends on the project. Using specialized hardware may require direct contact to set the

(continued)

Table 7.2 (continued)

Control mode	Control practices for agile software development	Possible adaptations
		hardware up for the client or the teams records a video presenting the current state of the project for the meeting
	Storyboards	Remote enactment by using digital services either separated, like Trello, or integrated in version control, like Azure DevOps
Self-control	Sustainable pace	Remote enactment through automated reports with warnings send to people, if certain thresholds are exceeded such as hours worked

may be useful or even desirable, yet, a high level of specialization is not worthwhile for developers as they need to be able to do multiple different roles (Conboy et al. 2011, pp. 51–52). Hence, there is no need for adaption for both top down work assignment and the inspection of documents to work for distributed teams as the position of team members as well as the creation of the documents is not affected by the pandemic. The cultural exchange workshops need to be adapted to work remotely as in the paper the workshop was held on site in Germany (Gregory et al. 2013, p. 1219).

The control practices with equivalent or similar practices in agile software development can also have different requirements than their agile counter parts. Using team feedback as an example, the practice can have different requirements when working remotely. While the control practice dialogue requires some method of communication and the practice group recognition has the need to form and articulate recognition of individual team members. The practice of team feedback could be implemented as a survey. Thus, it could either by anonymous or transparent, depending on the subject and the team's needs. In a similar vein, progress reports known in traditional software development have evolved into burndown charts and the sprint review meetings known in agile software development. While the practices are comparable between both methods, the practices still have different needs. For example, sprint review meetings need different tools due to its increased complexity. In part, the complexity stems from a focus on individuals (Beck et al. 2001).

The control practice of behavior and reward could not clearly be assigned to any method. The practice was mentioned in a paper that studied traditional development teams (Kirsch 1996, p. 9), but it was also mentioned in a study investigation agile software development teams (Remus et al. 2016, p. 20). In the latter, behavior control was only tested by the adherence to the prescribed behaviors, but its influence toward rewards and sanctions was not discussed. However, the practice seems to fit the focus on individuals known from the agile manifesto. Given this discrepancy, I could not clearly assign this practice to either development method. In practice, teams struggle to implement it in a remote working environment as the adherence to predefined behaviors is not incentivized. The link between outcomes and rewards is found in articles studying either traditional software development (Kirsch 2004, p. 385) or agile software development (Maruping et al. 2009, p. 396). Assuming a team uses version control like Git to tract source code changes and commits (Software Freedom Conservancy), this control practice is usable. Table 7.3 provides an overview of the identified control practices with their suggested adaptation.

Discussion

Based on my review of the literature, I identify three main avenues for future research:

- Socializing between team members is a challenge during COVID-19 and provides an avenue future research. Given the global nature of software development in conjunction with the different cultural backgrounds of team members, more questions arise. For example: How can we harmonize different client and vendor cultures given the restriction of COVID-19 pandemic?
- Clan Control requires further investigation in the context of a global pandemic. We need to better understand how the changes to the development processes affect the values, norms, and beliefs. Also, how the restrictions affect the effectiveness of control practices used to enact clan control remains unclear. For example: Suffers the effectiveness, remains it the same or does it grow due to relative isolation of team members?
- Behavioral changes of the team caused by remote or co-located members is another interesting area. Differences may have long-term effects toward the utilization of certain control modes. Do shifting control modes change behavior patterns of developers? Can teams maintain performance while changing control modes due to COVID-19?

These tentative conclusions should be interpreted in light of limitations. First, this study did not identify all possibly relevant articles. It might be that a relevant article was not sampled, despite our efforts to avoid this. Second, this article focuses on control practices as an umbrella term. As such, a term captures multiple practices at once, that other studies may investigate in further depth. Third, the study applies a broad categorization into traditional versus agile software development. A more fine-granular perspective may shed further light onto the literature. Fourth, I did not investigate the connection between control modes and control practices. A study of this area may reveal possible ways on whether the enactment of control modes with certain control practices is more effective, than with others. Fifth, the exclusion of the input control mode from the control practices, which has excluded some control practices.

Table 7.3 Overview of control practices and possible adaptations for use in traditional software development

Control mode	Control practices for traditional software development	Possible adaptations
Behavior control	Formal communication plan	Adapting communication services in use, for example, by setting up slack channels with system access privileges
	Predefined behaviors	Checking adherence after the fact, or using surveillance data, for example, via screen capture
	Reflection-in-action sessions	Remote enactment by using video conference services
	Replay session	Remote enactment by using screen capturing software
	Role clarification	Remote enactment by using access/viewing/changing rights for code or data
	Top down work assignment	Remote enactment via digital services to track tasks and allowing leaders to assign owners for each task
	Walkthroughs	Remote enactment by using video conference and screensharing software. Additional recording equipment, such as cameras, might be needed
Clan control	Commitment to the clan	Adaptation of rituals—for example, joint breaks and chats via video conference software—and norms to the remote environment
	Common understanding workshops	Remote enactment by using video conference services, prerecorded videos or Q&A sessions
	Culture and norms of the organization	Remote enactment is possible depending on the culture and norms. For example, the norm of excess work hours might be gamified using a digital leaderboards by hours worked
	Feedback from team members	Remote enactment by either an anonymous feedback system or additional feedback component in regular meetings
	Intercultural workshops	Remote enactment by using video conference services
	Peer pressure	Remote enactment via positive reinforcement during meetings, for example, praising team members that committed a significant amount of code
	Social events	Varies with purpose. For example, for socialization between team members, a remote enactment might be a virtual board game night. For information exchange, a remote enactment via video conference software using breakout rooms in order to facilitate also private discussions
	Socialization activities outside of work	Adaptation vary with the type of activity. Board game nights can be done virtually with software such as tabletop simulator. Get togethers can be organized using video conference software, where everyone brings a drink by herself

(continued)

Table 7.3 (continued)

Control mode	Control practices for traditional software development	Possible adaptations
	Team building sessions	Adaptation to remote enactment via digital media like cooperative video games, where communication and cooperation are required to advance, for example, Portal 2
Outcome control	Documentation	Remote enactment by using online word processing software or exchange via web services
	Formal daily meetings	Remote enactment via video conference software
	Progress reports	Using digital services that allow clients to see the current state of the project and the adherence to the project timeline
	Project plan	Remote enactment by using online word processing software in combination with video conference software to enable cooperative creation with all required team members
	Testing deliverables	Remote enactment by using version control systems
	Tracking goals and milestones	Remote enactment via digital services, like Trello only for the development practice
	Use of project management software templates	Adaptation to online accessible versions of the project management software, allowing the required personal a remote access

Conclusion

Findings from a review of 25 journal articles are presented about control of software development teams. The articles were analyzed using concept matrix in terms of control modes, control practices as well as software development method. The results offer a list of control practices, their possible adaptation during COVID-19 and identifies practices that cannot be enacted during COVID-19. The adaptations are only proposal that have not been empirically verified. Rather, they are only conjectures based on the purpose of the control practices as well as on the definitions of the control practices by for example the Agile Alliance in the "Agile Glossary" (Agile Alliance). Overall, we present three key findings:

- Many of the **control practices are usable despite the pandemic**. These include project plans, the use of predefined outcomes and other control practices for which it is possible to check adherence after the fact. Self-management and self-control do not require any adaption to work for distributed teams.
- Some **control practices require adaptation**. Control practices that cannot be used as is, often work in a remote setting using video conferencing services. Irrespective of the adaptation, it is important to ensure the controls purpose remains intact. This tasks rests with controller. For example, they have to ensure that the daily standup does not devolve into a discussion meeting.

- Some **control practices may not be applicable** to the COVID-19 situation or their effects in this context remains unclear. For example, socialization activities outside of the work or workshops might be difficult to implement and could have less impact that face-to-face interactions.

References

Agile Alliance. *Agile glossary*. Retrieved from https://www.agilealliance.org/agile101/agile-glossary/

Agile Alliance. *Planning Poker*. Retrieved from https://www.agilealliance.org/glossary/poker/

Agile Alliance. *Scrum*. Retrieved from https://www.agilealliance.org/glossary/scrum/

Beck, K., Beedle, M., van Bennekum, A., Cockburn, A., Cunningham, W., Fowler, M., & Thomas, D. (2001). *Manifesto for agile software development*. Retrieved from http://agilemanifesto.org/

Brhel, M., Meth, H., Maedche, A., & Werder, K. (2015). Exploring principles of user-centered agile software development: A literature review. *Information and Software Technology, 61*, 163–181. https://doi.org/10.1016/j.infsof.2015.01.004.

Choudhury, V., & Sabherwal, R. (2003). Portfolios of control in outsourced software development projects. *Information Systems Research, 14*(3), 291–314. https://doi.org/10.1287/isre.14.3.291.16563.

Chua, Lim, Soh, & Sia (2012). Enacting clan control in complex IT projects: A social capital perspective. *MIS Quarterly, 36*(2), 577–600. https://doi.org/10.2307/41703468

Conboy, K., Coyle, S., Wang, X., & Pikkarainen, M. (2011). People over process: Key challenges in agile development. *IEEE Software, 28*(4), 48–57. https://doi.org/10.1109/MS.2010.132.

Dreesen, T., & Schmid, T. (2018). Do as you want or do as you are told? Control vs. autonomy in agile software development teams. In T. Bui (Ed.), *Proceedings of the Annual Hawaii International Conference on System Sciences, Proceedings of the 51st Hawaii International Conference on System Sciences* (pp. 4815–4824). Hawaii International Conference on System Sciences. https://doi.org/10.24251/HICSS.2018.606

Gregory, R. W., & Keil, M. (2014). Blending bureaucratic and collaborative management styles to achieve control ambidexterity in IS projects. *European Journal of Information Systems, 23*(3), 343–356. https://doi.org/10.1057/ejis.2013.3.

Gregory, R. W., Beck, R., & Keil, M. (2013). Control balancing in information systems development offshoring projects. *MIS Quarterly, 37*(4), 1211–1232. https://doi.org/10.25300/MISQ/2013/37.4.10.

Harris, M. L., Collins, R. W., & Hevner, A. R. (2009). Control of flexible software development under uncertainty. *Information Systems Research, 20*(3), 400–419. https://doi.org/10.1287/isre.1090.0240.

Henderson, J. C., & Lee, S. (1992). Managing I/S design teams: A control theories perspective. *Management Science, 38*(6), 757–777. https://doi.org/10.1287/mnsc.38.6.757.

Highsmith, J. (2001). *History: The agile manifesto*. Retrieved from http://agilemanifesto.org/history.html

Huber, T. L., Fischer, T. A., Dibbern, J., & Hirschheim, R. (2013). A process model of complementarity and substitution of contractual and relational governance in IS outsourcing. *Journal of Management Information Systems, 30*(3), 81–114. https://doi.org/10.2753/MIS0742-1222300304.

Jaworski, B. J. (1988). Toward a theory of marketing control: Environmental context, control types, and consequences. *Journal of Marketing, 52*(3), 23–39. https://doi.org/10.1177/002224298805200303.

Keil, M., Rai, A., & Liu, S. (2013). How user risk and requirements risk moderate the effects of formal and informal control on the process performance of IT projects. *European Journal of Information Systems, 22*(6), 650–672. https://doi.org/10.1057/ejis.2012.42.
Kirsch, L. J. (1996). The Management of Complex Tasks in organizations: Controlling the systems development process. *Organization Science, 7*(1), 1–21.
Kirsch, L. J. (1997). Portfolios of control modes and IS Project Management. *Information Systems Research, 8*(3), 215–239. https://doi.org/10.1287/isre.8.3.215.
Kirsch, L. J. (2004). Deploying common systems globally: The dynamics of control. *Information Systems Research, 15*(4), 374–395. https://doi.org/10.1287/isre.1040.0036.
Kirsch, L. J., Sambamurthy, v., Ko, D.-G., & Purvis, R. L. (2002). Controlling information systems development projects: The view from the client. *Management Science, 48*(4), 484–498. https://doi.org/10.1287/mnsc.48.4.484.204.
Levy, Y., & Ellis, T. J. (2006). A systems approach to conduct an effective literature review in support of information systems research. *Informing Science: The International Journal of an Emerging Transdiscipline, 9*, 181–212. https://doi.org/10.28945/479.
Maruping, L. M., Venkatesh, V., & Agarwal, R. (2009). A control theory perspective on agile methodology use and changing user requirements. *Information Systems Research, 20*(3), 377–399. https://doi.org/10.1287/isre.1090.0238.
Microsoft. (2019, May 25). *What are the features in Azure DevOps?* Retrieved from https://docs.microsoft.com/en-us/azure/devops/user-guide/alm-devops-features?view=azure-devops
Microsoft. Visual Studio Live Share: Real-time collaborative development. Retrieved from https://visualstudio.microsoft.com/de/services/live-share/
Nerur, S., Mahapatra, R., & Mangalaraj, G. (2005). Challenges of migrating to agile methodologies. *Communications of the ACM, 48*(5), 73–78. https://doi.org/10.1145/1060710.1060712.
Nidumulo, S. R., & Subramani, M. R. (2003). The matrix of control: combining process and structure approaches to managing software development. *Journal of Management Information Systems, 20*(3), 159–196. https://doi.org/10.1080/07421222.2003.11045774.
Ouchi, W. G. (1979). A conceptual framework for the design of organizational control mechanisms. *Management Science, 25*(9), 833–848. https://doi.org/10.1287/mnsc.25.9.833.
Ouchi, W. G. (1980). Markets, bureaucracies, and clans. *Administrative Science Quarterly, 25*(1), 129–141. https://doi.org/10.2307/2392231.
Persson, J. S., Mathiassen, L., & Aaen, I. (2012). Agile distributed software development: Enacting control through media and context. *Information Systems Journal, 22*(6), 411–433. https://doi.org/10.1111/j.1365-2575.2011.00390.x.
Remus, U., Wiener, M., Saunders, C., Mähring, M., & Kofler, M. (2016). Control modes versus control styles: Investigating ISD project control effects at the individual level. In P. J. Ågerfalk, N. Levina, & S. S. Kien (Eds.), *ICIS 2016 Proceedings, Proceedings of the International Conference on Information Systems – Digital Innovation at the Crossroads* (pp. 1–21). AIS electronic library.
Software Freedom Conservancy. About: Data Assurance. Retrieved from https://git-scm.com/about/info-assurance
Software Freedom Conservancy. About: Branching and Merging. Retrieved from https://git-scm.com/about/branching-and-merging
Srivastava, S. C., & Teo, T. S. H. (2012). Contract performance in offshore systems development: Role of control mechanisms. *Journal of Management Information Systems, 29*(1), 115–158. https://doi.org/10.2753/MIS0742-1222290104
Teasley, S. D., Covi, L. A., Krishnan, M. S., & Olson, J. S. (2002). Rapid software development through team collocation. *IEEE Transactions on Software Engineering, 28*(7), 671–683. https://doi.org/10.1109/TSE.2002.1019481.
Tiwana, A. (2008). Does technological modularity substitute for control? A study of alliance performance in software outsourcing. *Strategic Management Journal, 29*(7), 769–780. https://doi.org/10.1002/smj.673.

Webster, J., & Watson, R. T. (2002). Analyzing the past to prepare for the future: Writing a literature review. *MIS Quarterly, 26*(2), 13–23.

Wiener, M., Mähring, M., Remus, U., & Saunders, C. (2016). Control configuration and control enactment in information systems projects: Review and expanded theoretical framework. *MIS Quarterly, 40*(3), 741–774. https://doi.org/10.25300/MISQ/2016/40.3.11.

Yoo, Y., Boland, R. J., Lyytinen, K., & Majchrzak, A. (2012). Organizing for innovation in the digitized world. *Organization Science, 23*(5), 1398–1408. https://doi.org/10.1287/orsc.1120.0771.

Chapter 8
How a New Venture Identified Digital Opportunities in the COVID-19 Crisis to Transform Their Business Model

Jana Teutenberg

Abstract The event market industry has decreased by the COVID-19 pandemic due to social distancing and the decline of public life. This essay examines a new venture operating in this market and particularly affected by the measures as it provides information about events in urban life. It is considered how the venture is identifying digital opportunities during crisis and transforming its existing business model. They used their digital platform capabilities during the pandemic to move from a "going out" to a "staying in" concept and to come to terms with social distancing measures. The venture has been very successful in adapting quickly to the new situation and offering both clients and artists a platform on which events can take place in a digital format, for example, via video streaming. Several strategy recommendations for new ventures were developed to learn from this case study how existing strategies can be adapted.

Keywords Business model transformation · New digital venture · Event market industry · Digital platform capability · Case study

Introduction

The COVID-19 outbreak has led to drastic measures being taken in many countries. The disease was first reported on in China at the end of December 2019 and was declared a pandemic and global health crisis in mid-March by the World Health Organization. Social life was restricted in almost all areas to prevent the virus from spreading. This has led to an exogenous shock in many economic sectors. Especially innovative new ventures are affected: they have to withstand various adversities, as very few young ventures have made preparations for such a crisis (Kuckertz et al. 2020).

J. Teutenberg (✉)
University of Cologne, Cologne, Germany
e-mail: jteutenb@smail.uni-koeln.de

C. Hovestadt et al. (eds.), *Digital Responses to Covid-19*, SpringerBriefs in Information Systems, https://doi.org/10.1007/978-3-030-66611-8_8

In addition, many political initiatives to support the economy during the pandemic are tailored towards established organizations. The focus is on maintaining the current status and less on the future, which is actually being promoted by the innovativeness of new ventures (Kuckertz et al. 2020). Particularly, ventures that were recently founded and are not thoroughly based on digital products and services are affected. Unlike large companies, new ventures have a lack of resources at their disposal and their liquidity is insufficient to survive for several months without significant income. In addition, quick and easy access to required loans is an issue (Turner and Akinremi 2020). Even if new ventures can successfully leverage their available resources, there is risk that growth and innovation potential will be limited or hindered (Kuckertz et al. 2020). Particularly, new ventures in the tourism or event industry are affected, as large events with many participants have been prohibited by many administrations and are assumed not take place in the near future (Ratten 2020). These industries must find a way to deal with the "new normal" lifestyle.

Therefore, it is worthwhile to look at how entrepreneurs manage the crisis and what concrete strategies they pursue to protect their venture. We will use a concrete example to show how a new venture can identify digital opportunities in the COVID-19 crisis and transform its existing business model. We will show that this transformation is economically viable in the long run and its outcomes are applicable after the crisis. Digital technology has proved a valuable enabler for new venture creation in different industries (von Briel et al. 2018). We seek to provide inspiration for other new ventures on how they can adapt their strategies during the crisis and how they can strengthen their preparedness for future crises.

Previous literature has mainly examined the impact of the COVID-19 crisis on new ventures and formulated general strategies on how small companies can survive the crisis and what policy measures should be implemented. Therefore, this paper will focus on concrete, practical strategies to not only survive the crisis but also to emerge from it with new ideas.

Prior Research

The challenges for new ventures created by the COVID-19 crisis and the resulting consequences and impacts are of growing interest in research but largely neglected in the public debate (Kuckertz et al. 2020). Emerald Publishing has launched a call for papers for "Journal of Entrepreneurship in Emerging Economies" on this topic in May 2020. Exemplary topics include "Doing business during pandemics: best practices and worst examples" and "Entrepreneurship and innovation in times of COVID-19 crisis" (Dvouletý et al. 2020).

Influence of COVID-19 on new ventures has already been identified as a cluster of research (Verma and Gustafsson 2020). The COVID-19 crisis can be characterized as a black swan event, which is a surprising and unpredictable event of great significance that causes dramatic changes in a political and economic environment (Kuckertz et al. 2020).

It is therefore interesting to look at innovative new ventures in crisis, as they are particularly sensitive to disruption. In the last week of March 2020 already 40% less new businesses were registered compared to the year before (Sedláček and Sterk 2020). Fewer Decreasing numbers of new ventures also directly reduce the number of new jobs. New ventures account for about three million jobs a year in contrast to existing companies that on average tend to shed jobs (Sedláček and Sterk 2020). In addition, the survival rate of new ventures, which generally lower than compared to established companies, will further decrease during crisis (Sedláček and Sterk 2020). In sum, innovation potential created by new ventures is threatened, which will have effects on areas that are dependent on innovation such as ecological sustainability. The impact of the crisis is therefore noticeable both in the short and long term (Naudé 2020).

Despite many political measures and loan schemes, many new ventures do not receive this help because they do not meet the traditional criteria for obtaining support such as a loan (Kuckertz et al. 2020). On the one hand, few new ventures have prepared themselves for crisis and previous crises have already shown that new ventures face dramatic consequences as cash flow is disrupted, there is less access to capital, and infrastructure problems arise. On the other hand, their specific characteristics offer new ventures opportunities to better respond to the crisis. Being innovative is an important prerequisite to be able to react to change (Kuckertz et al. 2020). They also have a higher flexibility due to their lower level of bureaucracy and limited social responsibility compliance (Alves et al. 2020).

The response strategy of small companies will continue to influence their performance after the crisis (Alves et al. 2020). Crisis management in an entrepreneurial context can be compared to the concept of bricolage, which is the construction or creation of a work from a diverse range of things that happen to be available. It makes more sense for new ventures to develop iterative and flexible approaches than to remain bound and rigid. Research on previous crises show that entrepreneurs have recognized opportunities offered by the available resources to increase resilience of their firms. Resilient firms use their available internal resources and call upon external resources to (re)form their business network (Kuckertz et al. 2020). According to Kuckertz et al. (2020) new ventures have generally two options to identify and pursue entrepreneurial opportunities in crisis: (1) adapt the business model and (2) restructure internally (see Fig. 8.1).

This concept, how a new venture works with its existing resources and uses the concept of bricolage, will be explored in detail in the following section. Since the pandemic and associated measures had critical impacts on industries that rely on physical contact, digital innovation may prove to be a valuable external enabler for new opportunities (von Briel et al. 2018). Innovation enabled through digital technologies can rapidly scale user bases for new ventures (Huang et al. 2017).

Previous research had a focus mainly on the ecological and political perspective of entrepreneurs' crisis management and less on the behavioral perspective (Ratten 2020). Therefore, the concrete behavior of a new venture in the crisis from the German event industry is now to be examined. This industry suffers from the fast lockdown as traditional events with larger numbers of participants cannot take place

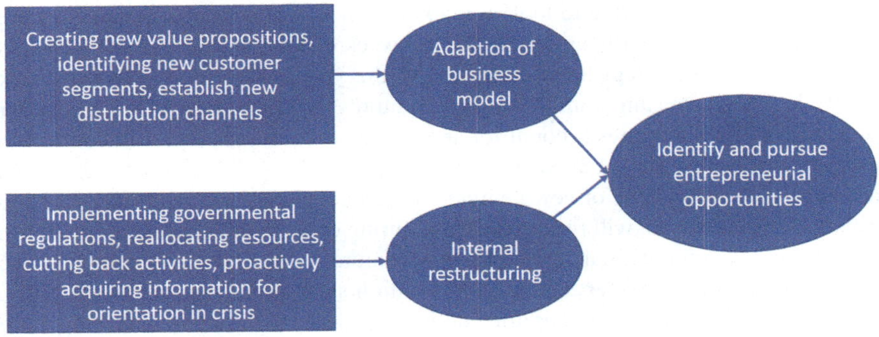

Fig. 8.1 Options to identify entrepreneurial opportunities (Kuckertz et al. 2020)

anymore. Therefore, they have to develop new types of events adapted to the crisis (Ratten 2020).

How "Rausgegangen" Effectively Used Bricolage to Manage the Crisis

Company Description

The German company "Rausgegangen" (eng. "Going out") was dramatically affected by the COVID-19 crisis and the associated "Stay-at-home" policy that was implemented, as the company name suggests.

In July 2015, the new venture started to provide at least three carefully researched, hand-picked and high-quality event tips (Rausgegangen 2020). Rausgegangen focuses on smaller and less known events instead of recommending large events, which people are generally aware of through other channels. In addition, the company has been offering self-organized events for some time now, such as the "Zusammen Leuchten" festival (eng. "Shine Together", a blend of music festival, live art, poetry, and workshops). All tips and tickets are also distributed via the Rausgegangen App (see Fig. 8.2). In addition to event tips, Rausgegangen offers recommendations for shops, restaurants, and cafés in the city. The app also offers a platform to connect with other users. The long-term goal is to create the largest independent event platform and to keep the community growing. This is to be achieved above all by integrating more cities and events. Therefore, the company developed a flexible backend that is able to serve every city in the world with the platform.

The first 13 months after the foundation were loss-making for the new venture (Rausgegangen 2020) and only in the last years the company could become profitable by selling its reach and by supporting the creation of events.

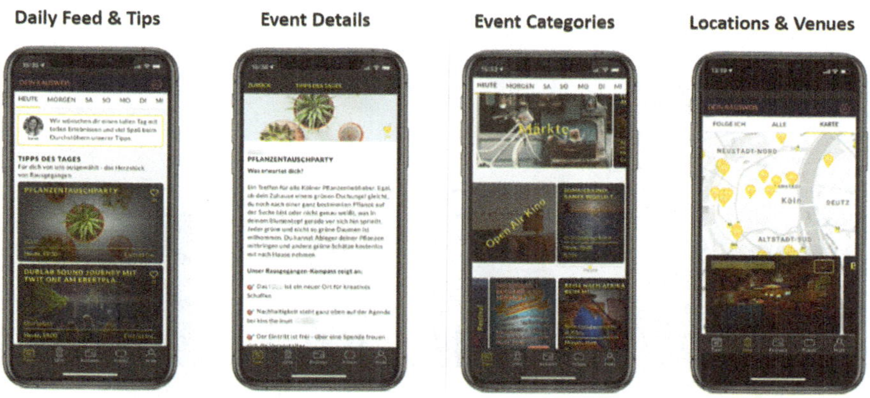

Fig. 8.2 Overview of Rausgegangen App Features. Screenshot by author from Rausgegangen Website by Rausgegangen (2020)

Although the new venture sells its services digitally, it is one of the companies that has been hit hard by the shutdowns caused by the COVID-19 crisis as being part of the event industry. Therefore, sources of income have almost come to a complete halt. Initially, events were canceled, no more cafés or restaurants could be visited and therefore customer were not able to benefit from the platform. Therefore, it was no longer worthwhile for sponsors and partners to advertise on the platform. Probably even many of the partners were also affected by the COVID-19 crisis, as most companies suffer from the restrictions.

In addition, event organizers no longer needed consultants for their events and would not use the company's services.

Similar to many other new ventures, this puts the company in a very difficult position because although it has grown in recent years, it has not yet made enough profit to survive for many months without a source of income. The company had started to develop further business ideas. However, while fighting for survival these innovations have been interrupted and may probably be implemented with some delay or not at all (reflecting the disrupted innovation growth of new ventures during crisis described by literature).

The company devised a plan to react to this new situation and launched the platform "Dringeblieben", (eng. "Stay Inside"). Dringeblieben is the answer of the new venture to cater cultural events to its users during the COVID-19 crisis. The new venture relied on its digital core competencies and digitized a large extent of previously physical offerings to make them available online. For this purpose, a platform was created that provides livestreams from the living rooms of artists, high-quality streams from the stages or edited news on the topic online (see Fig. 8.3). Many other cities were also integrated, in addition to Cologne and Munich, which were previously covered by Rausgegangen.

The company itself refers to the platform as a "digital gold mine" and explains that the service is intended to offer an alternative to the likes of Twitch and

Fig. 8.3 Dringeblieben platform. Screenshot by author from Dringeblieben Website by Dringeblieben (2020)

Fig. 8.4 Dringeblieben stream chat. Screenshot by author from Dringeblieben Website by Dringeblieben (2020)

YouTube. The claim is not to replace concerts or theatre with the digital service, but to offer solidarity to people and cultural communities in times of isolation and social distancing. Artists who also suffer economically due to the cancellation of all events and performances can be supported by putting support tickets on sale. Users can get in touch with the artist directly through an integrated chat (see Fig. 8.4).

Every user can create his own profile and join the community. Thus, new digital ways of generating revenue for the cultural scene in Germany are achieved. In the first 7 weeks, the company was able to broadcast approximately 1300 streams that reached 1.7 million clicks. As a result, over 240,000 euros were raised for the cultural scene. To date, the platform has shown a steady growth in streaming offerings and income for the company.

This shows the resounding success of the company's digital transformation and it is therefore interesting to look at the company's exact strategies and examine the benefits that users and partners have derived from this. We derive general recommendations for action for other new ventures.

The Venture's Strategic Pillars for Handling the Crisis

Flexibility

The new venture exploited one of its advantages over large companies: flexibility. Right at the beginning of the crisis, the entrepreneurs launched the platform within a few weeks in March, thus pre-empting all competition. Large companies working in the same industry, such as Eventim, which also sell tickets and promote events, could not adapt with such flexibility and did not change their strategy or developed their own response to the COVID-19 crisis. Instead they started to link to other platforms with online concerts, among others even "Dringeblieben" (Eventim 2020).

Relationships and Cooperation

The new venture has taken advantage of the relationships it has built up with the cultural scene over the last 5 years since its inception and has integrated many partners who were previously integrated on the platform into the new platform as well. This has two advantages for the company. On the one hand, it maintains and stabilizes the relationship with the partners and can continue to work with them after the crisis and, on the other hand, they were able to offer a wide range of different concerts, readings or workshops within a very short time. In addition, it has taken advantage of its relationships with similar companies and together they have been able to offer a wide range of events. For example, the initiative Culture Stream Cologne (Cologne 2020) offered a pay package for the Cologne club culture and a share of the income from the streams on Dringeblieben goes to this package.

Integration of New Sales Markets

The company already had plans to integrate further cities on the platform and thus to reach more users. To this end, plans were already made at the beginning of the year to buy up the insolvent young venture "Ask Helmut" in order to gain Berlin as a major market (Gründerszene 2020). Therefore, the company took advantage of the COVID-19 crisis and accelerated the process in which they built the new platform together with AskHelmut and thus were able to win the platform's users. In addition, they have gained new partners and have thus integrated a total of 27 cities to date. With the support of the Ministry of Economic Affairs, Innovation, Digitalization and Energy of the State of NRW and CREATIVE.NRW, they are able to start off in NRW in particular.

Fig. 8.5 Dringeblieben support tickets. Screenshot by author from Dringeblieben Website by Dringeblieben (2020)

Technology and Independence

The platform is based on its own video player and is therefore independent of YouTube, Twitch or other video providers. It also offers the creation of a community that is not based on the algorithms of Instagram and Co. Every artist can create his own profile, which users can bookmark. In addition, there is an own framework to collect financial support. The artists can decide what kind of support they want to offer and thus personalize their offerings (Fig. 8.5). For example, artists can choose to make their streams only accessible via payment and offer payed subscriptions.

Advantages of the Dringeblieben Platform

Advantages for Users

The new platform offers various advantages to users. The members of the "Rausgegangen" community consist of culture and music enthusiasts who are no longer able to pursue their passion in the COVID-19 crisis. Via the platform they can counteract boredom and isolation and pursue their hobby in a new digital way. In addition, they have the opportunity to support their favorite artists and venues so that they can surpass the crisis. At the same time, they can reach out to artists and interact with them via chat. This possibility does not exist at live events for most fans.

Another advantage is the possibility to discover new things because the user can discover streams of local artists from far away at any time from home without travel time. This enables attending remote events not accessible in the past, for example, during work weeks. Furthermore, users can also explore streams even when in doubt whether they suit the taste. The fact that most offered streams are free of cost, increases the willingness of users to experience something more unusual.

Furthermore, users who were not able to attend offline events before, due to financial limitations or health issues, can also use these streams. These advantages could motivate users to remain a part of the community in the long run.

Advantages for Partners

The platform offers the various artists, musicians, locations and other providers the opportunity to continue performing and thereby reduce the losses caused by cancelled performances. In addition, there is the chance to reach new target groups and increase the level of awareness. This can lead to new offers after the crisis. Furthermore, artists' traveling efforts and costs are reduced. Many artists travel throughout the year to perform at live shows. Currently, they can entertain their fans from home and thus reduce financial strains as well as stress. Artists can also solidarize with other artists and venues, for example, by donating a part of their income to cultural support programmes.

New and very unknown artists can also benefit from the online stream as they are more likely to be able to perform in front of a large audience. Overall, there is less risk and effort for the organizers of events.

Opportunities After the Crisis

The company has already developed further ideas on how to continue to drive the digital business after the crisis. The goal was formulated to develop the technical backbone of the new digital cultural scene and to open new possibilities for the cultural scene. It is not the goal to replace the offline experience. But the entrepreneurs see a new opportunity in the digital event world as it will enable them to break away from the structures and sales dependencies of the offline world.

They want to provide further payment models such as subscriptions, micropayments, crowdfunding concerts, or the closer involvement of industry partners. As a medium-term goal, they seek to integrate video advertising so that the artist can play advertising if desired and can also finance his performance. In general, communication through the chat is to be further improved and further community advantages expanded. In the long term, it is an important goal to attract and integrate additional artists and partners into the platform. Many users become aware of the platform because of performances of artists they follow.

Through the diversification and combination of the digital and offline world, the company can emerge stronger from the COVID-19 crisis. It can continue to serve its loyal and newly acquired customers. In addition to the two traditional sources of revenue (i.e., selling tickets and offering platform reach to partners), the crisis has created the opportunity to a substantial third source of revenue.

Lessons Learned: Strategy Recommendations for New Ventures

From the strategy of "Rausgegangen", general recommendations for other new ventures can be derived on how they can overcome the COVID-19 crisis and develop new strategies that can help them to move forward in the long run even after the crisis.

1. **Use core competencies**: The new venture should focus on what core competencies it has and work out how they can change them to be able to offer them during the COVID-19 crisis. They need to consider which values are important to the customer and what would make them use the company's product or service during the COVID-19 crisis.
2. **Technology:** Despite the need for rapid restructuring to counteract the loss of revenue as quickly as possible, the technologies used should be well thought-out and long-term, using sensible technologies that can be retained after the crisis and do not require further restructuring. In addition, users should be kept satisfied to retain them, and to this end, the online presence should be as user-friendly as possible.
3. **New ideas:** Plans that were developed before the COVID-19 crisis should not be postponed. In short-term, e-evaluating whether these plans can be implemented in an adapted form to help navigate through crisis is necessary. At the same time, it is necessary to consider whether implementation is possible in the near future to keep the innovative edge for new ventures.
4. **Supporters:** During the crisis a lot of organizations have emerged that focus on making a contribution together and support each other. A new venture should not only fight its way through the crisis but should also look for supporters and partners and thus make use of each other's reach.
5. **Set goals**: The new venture should not only optimize its strategy for the COVID-19 crisis but set long-term goals. Developing ideas that are sustainable after the crisis is critical. It could be fatal to think that going back to normal after crisis and stick to old processes is viable. Ideally, long-term goals interweave old and new strategies to a mixture that offers sustainability and flexibility to the company.

Conclusions

Even if most innovative new ventures do not directly address health crisis concerns such as medication and diagnosis, they are nevertheless an important part of a vital business environment in the long term. From an economic point of view, new ventures can serve as catalyst to show up ways for economic growth, innovation, and creating jobs during crisis. As an importing factor for overcoming the crisis, new ventures such as Rausgegangen keep the cultural offerings alive, which can provide people with distraction and hope during crisis.

Despite the great burden of the COVID-19 crisis for new ventures, new opportunities can also arise. It can be seen that the strategies chosen by the new venture are in line with the theoretical recommendations of Kuckertz et al. (2020), as the company has created new value propositions and gained new customers through new channels. The new venture has practically implemented the point "adaptation of the business model" (Kuckertz et al. 2020, p. 4).

In this paper, the focus was on one concrete example and thus on a specific industry that was particularly affected during the crisis. Moreover, it has been demonstrated that a new venture is not necessarily dependent on government support but can also survive the crisis by its own efforts.

The clear advantage for small new ventures is their flexibility, which enables them to react quickly and innovatively to changes in their environment. This example shows that by adapting their strategy appropriately, new ventures can emerge as stronger from crisis. After all, they have proven that they can be resilient and also be prepared for coming crises and find the right strategy to respond to them.

Since it makes sense for a new venture to not immediately give up the strategy that was developed for the crisis, but to continue to develop it nevertheless, it is possible that the next crisis will not affect them to the same extent as the current one.

For future investigations, it will be useful to examine additional new ventures, in different industries and with different products and services, in order to develop further strategy proposals. It could be examined, for example, whether other new ventures also apply a similar strategy and adapt their business model, or whether they use other strategies to retain the existing model. It is useful to compare different strategies to develop best practices. These practices can serve as an inspiration for different new ventures to choose their future strategies.

Furthermore, it could be examined whether the companies after the crisis actually combine the developed strategy with their old strategy to achieve new growth and to be prepared for further crises.

Currently, only the short-term effects of the chosen strategies can be examined. In the long term, it should be observed whether the strategies are still effective after the crisis. The strategies can be tested to see if they are indeed effective and adaptable in a potential next crisis, or if the strategies need to be adjusted again.

References

Alves, J. C., Lok, T. C., Luo, Y., & Hao, W. (2020). Crisis management for small business during the COVID-19 outbreak: Survival. *Resilience and Renewal Strategies of Firms in Macau*. https://doi.org/10.21203/rs.3.rs-34541/v1

Cologne, C. S. (2020). *Culture stream Cologne website*. Retrieved from https://www.culture-stream.cologne/

Dringeblieben. (2020). *Dringeblieben website*. Retrieved from https://dringeblieben.de/

Dvouletý, O., de Arroyabe, J. C. F., & Mustafa, M. (2020). Entrepreneurship during the times of COVID-19 pandemic: Challenges and consequences. *Journal of Entrepreneurship in Emerging Economies*.

Eventim. (2020). Retrieved from https://www.eventim.de/magazin/rock-pop/zuhausekonzerte-die-livestreams-aus-den-wohnzimmern-der-stars/

Gründerszene. (2020). *Eventseite Ask Helmut ist insolvent und steht vor einer Übernahme*. Retrieved from https://www.gruenderszene.de/business/ask-helmut-insolvenz-uebernahme

Huang, J., Henfridsson, O., Liu, M. J., & Newell, S. (2017). Growing on steroids: Rapidly scaling the user base of digital ventures through digital innovation. *Mis Quarterly, 41*(1), 301–314.

Kuckertz, A., Brändle, L., Gaudig, A., Hinderer, S., Reyes, C. A. M., Prochotta, A., & Berger, E. S. (2020). Startups in times of crisis–A rapid response to the COVID-19 pandemic. *Journal of Business Venturing Insights, 13*(1), 1–13.

Naudé, W. (2020). Entrepreneurial recovery from COVID-19: Decentralization, democratization, demand, distribution, and demography. *IZA Discussion Paper No. 13436*. Retrieved from https://ssrn.com/abstract=3643200

Ratten, V. (2020). Coronavirus and international business: An entrepreneurial ecosystem perspective. *Thunderbird International Business Review, 62*(5), 629–634.

Rausgegangen. (2020). *Rausgegangen website*. Retrieved from https://rausgegangen.de/

Sedláček, P., & Sterk, V. (2020). Startups and employment following the COVID-19 pandemic: A calculator. *CEPR Discussion Paper*. Retrieved from http://users.ox.ac.uk/~econ0506/Documents/StartupCalculator/StartupCalculator_WP.pdf

Turner, J., & Akinremi, T. (2020). *The business effects of pandemics–A rapid literature review*. Enterprise Research Centre. Retrieved from https://www.enterpriseresearch.ac.uk/wp-content/uploads/2020/04/ERC-Insight-The-business-effects-of-pandemics-%E2%80%93-a-rapid-literature-review-Final.pdf

Verma, S., & Gustafsson, A. (2020). Investigating the emerging COVID-19 research trends in the field of business and management: A bibliometric analysis approach. *Journal of Business Research, 118*, 253–261.

von Briel, F., Davidsson, P., & Recker, J. (2018). Digital technologies as external enablers of new venture creation in the IT hardware sector. *Entrepreneurship Theory and Practice, 42*(1), 47–69.

Chapter 9
Development of an Application to Manage Hygiene Measures in the Grocery Retail Sector

Shanice Casado Gracia

Abstract Managing the hygiene measures in the grocery retail sector has gained more and more importance during the COVID-19 pandemic. The sector faces a great challenge to keeping further spread as low as possible while not restricting people in their daily routines. Research focuses on what restrictions have been taken into action. However, less attention has been paid on the effects of the shopping experience of customers. The author develops an application that allows the reduction of the number of people in a shop while at the same time avoiding long queues and loss of time, exploiting the possibilities of digital technologies. Problems that have not yet been resolved despite hygiene measures and their effects are discussed. The developed application provides a basis for further development and conception of prototypes using digital technologies.

Keywords Application development · Digital technology · Hygiene measure · Grocery retail sector · Pandemic

Introduction

The COVID-19 outbreak has changed our daily life around the world. Because of its rapid nature of spreading, it has developed into a global pandemic in a very short time (WHO 2020).

Until now, it has been assumed that the main source of disease spreading within the population is due to a droplet infection. Dissemination occurs directly from person to person in close physical interaction (Jayaweera et al. 2020). Depending on the number of infections, governments worldwide issued hygiene rules, distance rules, contact blocks up to complete curfews to reduce any risk of infection. The measures of the government also had major impact on the daily lives of people. One of these affected and disrupted practices is grocery shopping (Lobach 2020).

S. Casado Gracia (✉)
University of Cologne, Cologne, Germany

C. Hovestadt et al. (eds.), *Digital Responses to Covid-19*, SpringerBriefs in Information Systems, https://doi.org/10.1007/978-3-030-66611-8_9

As infection rates have reached record highs in April 2020, the German government took strict measures to prevent health care system overload and drastic rise in mortality rates. Beside social distancing, one of the measures, for example, in the state of North Rhine-Westphalia was the closedown of all shops selling non-essential goods for a couple of weeks. That means that all shops that are not selling articles for daily use such as hygiene products, food products or pharmaceuticals had to close. After several weeks, they were allowed to reopen, but only under certain hygiene conditions.

This had a major economic impact on the retail sector. In particular, many private shops have struggled for their existence and they are afraid of another lock-down, and with them the employees whose jobs are in danger (Nicola et al. 2020). Until now, 20,000 shops have already been closed only in the United Kingdom (Munbodth 2020).

During times of lock-down, grocery stores had to remain open to meet the basic needs of the people. This does not mean, however, that these stores have a lower risk of infection. Because of COVID-19 can spread quickly through close physical interaction also supermarkets are a very risky place for spreading the virus (Sudrajat 2020). Therefore, personal contact points should be avoided as far as possible. There are already initial legal requirements to limit the number of people per square meter in publicly accessible areas. For example, the government of North Rhine-Westphalia stipulates that only one customer per ten square meters of shop space should be allowed in the shops in order to reduce the risk of infection (BGWH 2020).

The shop space thus includes all areas of a business which are accessible to customers, in which goods are offered and which are spatially and functionally related to the sales process apart from pure storage areas, staff rooms or the customer toilet (Köhler and Klett 2016). However, this calculation does not take into account the fact that especially in supermarkets there are very narrow aisles because of the many shelves on both sides and the behavior of customers in stressful situations.

Because people have had little to no experience with worldwide pandemics, they reacted insecure and panicky. This fear is also reflected in their shopping behavior. They buy large stocks because they are afraid of a food shortage. This results in overcrowded supermarkets where people hectically reach for the food on the shelves and do not pay attention on the distance. As a result, customers are under time pressure because they want to get out of the store as soon as possible to avoid any close contact with others (Lobach 2020). One option would be to let less people into the shops at the same time. However, long waiting times for essential goods in supermarkets is not feasible. This situation brings the grocery shopping about to be perceived as an unpleasant chore (Lobach 2020).

In order to keep the risk in grocery stores as low as possible, there are some rules that will be still maintained after the critical phase when the number of infections are rising.

Therefore, the grocery sector has to change its service system in order to minimize the risk of the spread of the virus while providing customers with the best possible shopping experience. Previous hygiene measures in shops did not rely on digital technologies although these technologies have proven their great potential in areas such as teaching (Reimers et al. 2020), diagnostics (Whitelaw et al. 2020) and remote working (Mukhopadhyay 2020).

Our goal is to use the possibilities of digital technologies to develop an application that allows reduction of the number of people in a shop while at the same time avoiding long queues and loss of time. To this end, we seek to support consumers in performing grocery shopping as an important part of their everyday routine as well as shopping for non-essentials that can be an important part of self-fulfillment.

State of the Literature

Research on the pandemic is in full swing. There is already a large number of scientific papers analyzing and forecasting the general impact of the pandemic. In particular, the use of digital technologies plays a major role in this pandemic (Fletcher and Griffith 2020). For example, digital technology is used for faster diagnosis, remote working in companies, to teach students at home, and tracking infection chains. However, research on how these technologies can be used in the retail sector is lagging behind (apart from the trend in online shopping). A foundation of research on how people handle their daily routines such as shopping during the pandemic and how they perceive the implemented hygiene measures is required (Lobach 2020).

Most of the research focus on what restrictions have been taken into action to manage the crisis. One study provides an overview of the main restrictions that are already taken by government of Australia (Beck and Hensher 2020). A more detailed overview of the situation, especially in supermarkets, is provided by a qualitative study (Lobach 2020). The authors investigate current measures in supermarkets in Sweden and the resulting change in shopping behavior. Most of measures in shops are analogue and not yet digital in nature.

Further studies also show that the measures that are based on digital technologies are rare in supermarkets and stores. One potential reason given for this is the fact that supermarkets and especially smaller stores are less digitally mature and therefore not able to integrate digital technologies in their organizational structure (Grashuis et al. 2020). Organizations with higher levels of digital maturity are generally more flexible to react to rapidly changing circumstances (Fletcher and Griffith 2020).

An example of this is the introduction of online shops (Bakibinga-Gaswaga et al. 2020). Several studies analyzed how online shopping has increased during the pandemic (Güsken et al. 2019). Authors discuss how customers react to the fact that supermarkets are also offering their food in online shops. However, even in time of the pandemic many consumers still exhibit a preference for the in-store purchasing (Grashuis et al. 2020). For older people, grocery shopping is an essential activity for social interacting (Grashuis et al. 2020).

Apart from the implementation of online shops, one digital measure was the development of a traffic light system (Lobach 2020; Connfair 2020). Traffic lights are located at the entrance of the shops and the system counts customers going in and out. Red light represents that the maximum number of customers is reached and further customers are prevented from entering until the light turns green again. The underlying technology is based on available systems developed prior to the pandemic (Garcia et al. 2013; Li et al. 2015; Conrad 1994). It was already used for large events to regulate and organize the flow of people with regard to safety and customer satisfaction to be realized at the same time, to collect data on visitor flows or simplify the scheduling of sales personnel (Garcia et al. 2013).

These automated admission systems with traffic lights enables the automated control of permissible capacity limits without exposing staff, customers or visitors to the risk of infection. At the same time, a total overview of capacities available online ensures an optimal distribution of visitor traffic (Connfair 2020).

Although this new technology supports compliance with the measures on the side of the retailers, the customer's view has not been addressed so far. Pandemic research focuses on the ability to take measure and manage the crisis from a health perspective not paying a lot of attention on how the individuals continue go about their everyday practices, such as grocery shopping (Lobach 2020; Beck and Hensher 2020; Pasco et al. 2020).

In evaluating whether a measure is successful or not, officials primary rely on reproduction rates of the infection describing how many people an infected person infects on average (RKI 2020). However, reproduction rates cannot assess how the measures affect people in their daily routines.

For this reason, it is worthwhile to look at the customer's side and develop an application in order to turn the shopping experience into something nice even during a pandemic.

Current Hygiene Measures and Their Impact on Customer Behavior

At the beginning it is necessary to analyses which problems occurr in the stores during the pandemic. For this purpose, we reviewed prior literature and conducted interviews. Five interviews were conducted with focus on the effects of hygiene measures in grocery stores. This enables comparing how the situation was perceived at the time of the outbreak, compared to the current situation and what has changed since then. The interviews will be conducted with volunteers at different ages.

Analysis of the interviews show that many different measures were taken in the shops to reduce the risk of infection. Meanwhile guidance in the form of visual signs was implemented in almost all shops to guide people during their shopping tour. The signs distributed in the shops explain how to behave correctly during the pandemic in multiple languages. Examples include notes indicating not to come into the shop if feeling ill, not shaking hands, sneezing into the arm crook, not to buy more than necessary, and to pay preferably contactless (Ebster and Garaus 2011). Markings on the floor remind customers to keep two meters distance from other. Furthermore, different grocery stores have introduced special opening hours only available for risk groups, hand sanitizers, plastic gloves, and glass walls at the cash desks (Lobach 2020; Desai 2020). One measure that all interviewees mentioned is the maximum number of people who can be in the shop at the same time. This number should not be exceeded.

There are three ways the shops currently handle this. The first option is that a staff member counts customers entering and leaving the shop. In case of multiple entrances, shops generally only use one entrance for easier customer counting. Interviewees note that this option generally reduces accessibility to the shop. For example, one respondent mentions, "I also liked to take the path through the store as a shortcut. Even if I wasn't looking for anything special to buy, I often saw something spontaneously and took it with me." Two others have confirmed this and also said that it would be inconvenient if only one entrance was open, because then sometimes they would have to walk around the whole store to get into it. This increases economic strains on shops in addition to the general decrease in shopping due to the crisis and the increase in staff cost to control shop entrances (Nicola et al. 2020).

The second option, which is also used by many shops, especially clothes shops and smaller shops, is to use shopping carts and baskets. These are located at the entrance of the shop with signs saying that customers may only enter the shop with a shopping cart or basket. If no cart or bag is available, customers have to wait until one is returned by a previous customer (and potentially cleaned before by the shop personnel).

One interviewee said "I would rather use my own bag, because I want to touch as few foreign objects as possible. It was also said that the virus may adhere to objects. These shopping carts and baskets are not disinfected. No one is paying attention to that.". Another interviewee said that she thinks it is very cumbersome to have to take an additional shopping cart: "I also find this annoying, when I go shopping with my husband I have to take my own trolley and my husband also, although the aisles in the supermarket are already very narrow anyway, you have even less space to move. I then push the empty shopping cart through the whole store, because of course we only use one. It's no fun shopping". Three interviewees mention that it is very annoying and time consuming when long queues form in front of the shops due to waiting customers. Almost all of the interviewees remarked that many people do not adhere to the procedures or that they sometimes also forget to take a basket and overlooked the signs.

Another option installed are the so-called entry traffic lights. This traffic light indicates whether people are allowed to enter the shop or not. When the maximum number is reached, the light turns red and customers have to wait until other customers leave the shop. When entrance is allowed again, the traffic light turns green. The traffic light contains a sensor that counts how many people pass by and can detect whether someone enters or leaves the shop. The interviewees were in general most positive about this option. They think it is good that they are not forced to take shopping carts or baskets. In addition, there is no need to fall back to a single entrance solution when using automated systems that can monitor several entrances simultaneously.

Almost all interviewees noted three major points of criticism. First, the long waiting times are in front of shops is perceived as an unnecessary loss of time. One even said that she had already given up shopping because she did not have time to queue. Another interviewee said that he had already been sent away because the queue was so long that he would not have been able to get in before the shop closes. Second, crowded shops are perceived as a health risk. Despite all the measures taken, too many customers are still being let in at the same time. This affects supermarkets in particular because despite the large store size, the aisles are very narrow, and the checkout area is also very narrow because of the shelves. At the cash desks there is then also a big crowd and long queues.

Third, interviewees report that an agitated atmosphere during the pandemic quickly leads to arguments inside the shops. Media has reported on arguments which have also ended violently. People are already stressed while experiencing an uncertain situation such as a pandemic (Aylott and Mitchell 1998) and the current shopping experience in the circumstances leads to additional stress. One interviewee said that he had experienced arguments over food such as who gets the last package of pasta.

Compared to the beginning of the pandemic, the interviewees report that in some cases the hygiene measures are less strictly enforced as in the beginning period. They reported on people who do not keep their distance and employees in the shops who do not wear their masks properly over their mouth. Carelessness may lead to higher infection rates and these stores signal higher infection risk, which may lead to fewer people who want to shop in these stores (Grashuis et al. 2020).

To counteract these issues, measures should be taken, which the customers do not perceive as a burden but as an aid. Precautionary measures taken by the stores can reduce the infection risk (Pasco et al. 2020).

To provide a solution to improve the shopping experience for customers during the pandemic and at the same time reduce the risk of infection, we develop a concept of an application in the following.

PlanYourShoppingSafe

I now introduce a concept for a mobile application for the smartphones and tablets called PlanYourShoppingSafe. The prototyped app is based on data that is provided by the Connfair's Customer Flow Control System, which we present in the first sub-section following (section "Connfairs Customer Flow Control System"). The developed prototype concept for the mobile app is presented in the second sub-section (section "Architecture of the Mobile App"). In the final subsection (section "Interaction Between PlanYourShoppingSafe and Connfair"), the interaction process between Confair and the mobile app is presented.

Connfairs Customer Flow Control System

The customer flow control system that is used for the prototype is offered by the company Connfair in cooperation with its strategic partner tec.direct IT Systems GmbH. Connfair specializes in automated entry and control systems. In 2016 Connfair developed for the first time a digital platform to bring the different parties of an event together centrally and to ensure an optimized digital process and information flow. The first modules for ticketing and admission management have been on the market since 2018 (Connfair 2020).

The companies Connfair and tec.direct entered into a strategic partnership in April 2020 to make a decisive contribution against the spread of COVID-19 and beyond by adapting the mobile entry system. Due to governmental regulations that formulate a maximum number of people allowed to in a shop at the same time, Connfair and tec-direkt have developed a joint solution approach. They developed an entrance system that automatically controls the permissible capacity by tracking every costumer who enters or leaves the shop by use of sensory traffic lights (Connfair 2020). Figure 9.1 visualizes an illustrative process flow when using a traffic light at a shop that has reached a maximum number of customers.

If the traffic light is red, the arriving customer is not allowed to enter the shop as the maximum number of customers has already been reached. If the customer would enter the store anyway, a loud warning signal would sound. The customer waits at the traffic light until another customer leaves the shop. The system recognizes without contact that a person has left the store and the traffic light switches to green. The customer can now enter the store. The server then checks whether the

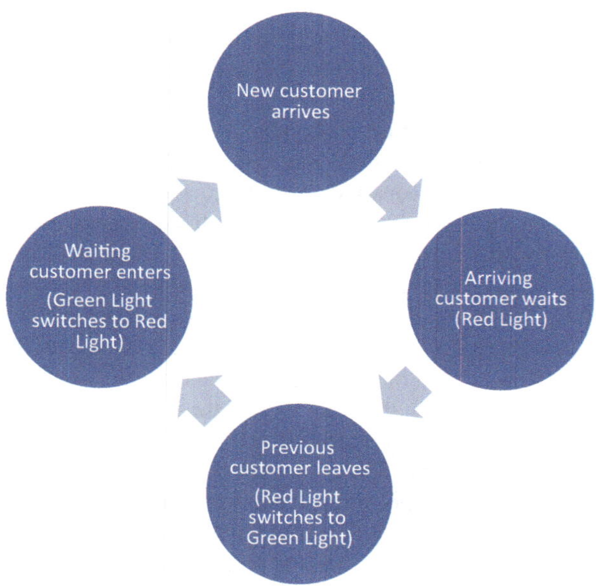

Fig. 9.1 Process flow of the counter system in a supermarket (Connfair 2020)

maximum number of shoppers has been reached and if so, switches the traffic light back to red. The entire process works without exposing staff and customers to the risk of infection due to physical interaction with the system.

Connfair's system does not only consist of a traffic light system, but it also offers an admin tool for supervising employees of the respective shop. The admin tool is a central web interface that allows to view data collected by the entrance control system and provides real-time visibility of the data. For example, the current workload and historical evaluations of the collected data can be viewed. In addition to user administration, it is also possible to conFig. system parameters such as the maximum number of customers allowed. Collected real-time data about the number of customers in the shop and also historical data is made available to the prototype.

Architecture of the Mobile App

The main functionality of the app is that customers can plan their shopping trip in advance using data from Connfair's traffic light system. As a counterpart to the admin page that Confair provides, which allows shops to monitor and manually adjust the maximum number of customers, PlanYourShoppingSafe is intended to be for the customer side.

The application connects to Connfair's traffic light system and also uses the sane data as that system. Additionally, it offers a user interface where users can plan their shopping in advance. The app receives all information about the current number of customers in the store in real-time, ensuring that the user can always interact with the system to review the current status.

Based on the findings, requirements for the application are developed. In order to provide a fundamental overview of the requirements, they are presented as a use case diagram (see Fig. 9.2).

Users are customers who plan a visit to the shop. A distinction is made between customers who plan their purchases from home and customers who are already in the city and spontaneously decided to go shopping at a store.

The application allows customers from home to plan their shopping trip. They can log into the app and view a selection of shops in their area but can also search for shops. They select the shop they want to visit. There they can check at what time the store has free capacity and choose an available time slot.

Furthermore, the app collects the data of the participating stores and gives an overview at what time the store was least visited in the past and based on that it gives a prediction when the store will be the least visited in the future. Another feature of the application is, that the customers can rate their shopping experience. This creates a competition between the shops.

To score superior ratings, the shops strive to implement the hygiene measures in the best possible way. It is challenging to offer a pleasant shopping experience while increasing people's safety and reducing the risk of infection.

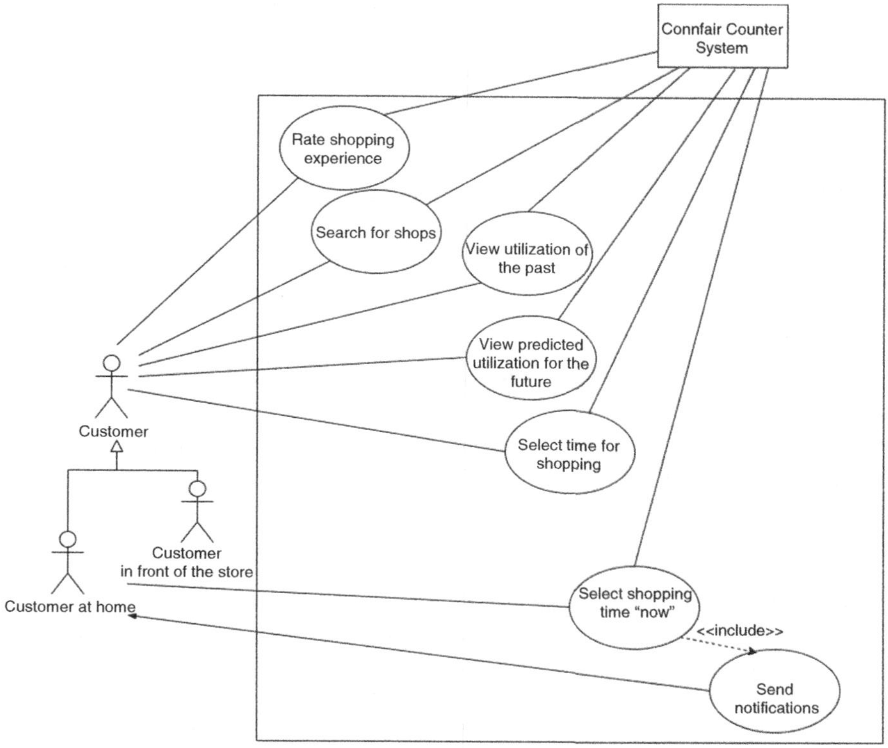

Fig. 9.2 Use case diagram of PlanYourShoppingSafe mobile app

If the customer is already in the near area, they can go directly to the shop and check if the maximum number of people has already been reached. The customers can recognize this by the installed traffic light from Connfair, which is placed at the entrance of the shop. If the light is green the customer can enter the shop. However, if the light is red the maximum number of people who can be in the store at the same time has already been reached. If the light is red, the customer does not have to wait in front of the store. They log into the app and note that they would like to enter the store, by selecting shopping time "now". Additionally, they can enter how many people are with them to ensure that they can visit in a group. The app creates a digital queue based on the first come first serve principle.

The time that the customer would normally have to wait in front of the store can now be used efficiently and other tasks in the surrounding area can be done first.

The application constantly receives information from Connfair when customers leave the shop.

Based on the current load and data collected from previous, the application calculates how long the waiting time will be until the customer have to come back to the store. The user can check this predicted time in real-time.

If two more customers have to leave the shop before the customer is allowed in, he will be informed that he can now go to the shop. After the user receives a notification that he can come back to the store, there will either be no waiting time at all or only a very short waiting time of a few minutes.

Due to the fact that there are very limited waiting times, the shops also have the possibility to reduce the maximum number of people so that there is no more crowding in the narrow aisles of the supermarket. This would reduce the risk of infection and at the same time make the shopping experience more pleasant for people.

Interaction Between PlanYourShoppingSafe and Connfair

To implement the PlanYourShoppingSafe Mobile App, a connection to the server of Connfair is required. To illustrate the interaction between the prototype and the Connfair Server, a sequence diagram is presented to visualize the information flow in Fig. 9.3.

The diagram illustrates the interaction between the application and the Connfair Server using the main functionality of PlanYourShoppingSafe.

The application establishes a constant connection to the Connfair Server to get the data about the current number of customers in the store in real-time. Received data is then continuously updated in the application to keep the customers up to date.

When the user selects a time for shopping, the application sends this request with the entered date to the Connfair server. The Connfair Server confirms that this time

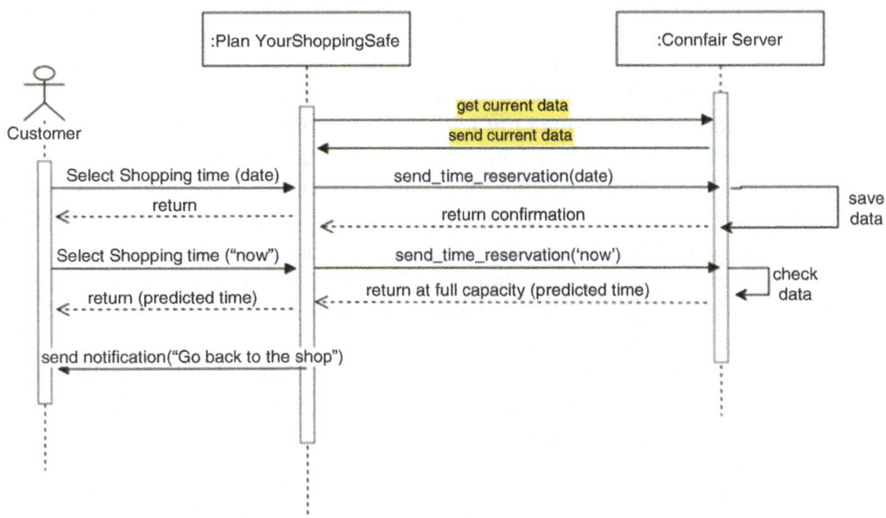

Fig. 9.3 Sequence diagram of interaction between prototype and the Connfair server

slot is still available, updates the workload for the transmitted date on the server, and sends a confirmation to the application. The application then sends a confirmation to the user. As the data is continuously updated, the app stores this new information.

In case the customer chooses "now" as shopping time, a request is also sent to the server. The server returns the message that the maximum number has been reached and based on the request it predicts a time how long it will take until the customer can enter the store, based on virtual queue. The Application updates this information and makes it available for the customer. If there are only two customers (this parameter is configurable by shop supervisors) left in the shop, the waiting customer is notified.

Preliminary Evaluation

To get a short initial evaluation of the idea, the concept of the prototype is presented to five interviewees of different ages. During the presentation, feedback was collected using the Thinking Aloud method (Nielsen 1993) and then evaluated. With this method, the interviewees stated aloud what they were thinking while they heard the description of concept of PlanYourShoppingSafe.

Feedback on the prototype was consistently positive. The interviewees commented expressions like "wow" or "cool" right at the beginning and said that it was "really a good idea". The interviewees were all of the opinion that the application addresses a problem that affects everyone who goes shopping during the pandemic. They especially like the fact that supermarkets, which are usually very crowded, have the possibility to reduce their maximum number of customers without having a negative effect on the customer. Interviewees were particularly positive about the distinction between planned and spontaneous visits.

Interviewees mentioned several aspects that could be implemented in the future (see Table 9.1 for an overview). The additional feature of being able to rate the stores was considered a good feature that the respondents would use. One interviewee reported that there are shops where the mask rules are not enforced strictly by

Table 9.1 Possible directions for further development of PlanYourShoppingSafe

Feature	Description
Hygiene rating for stores	Customers can rate stores depending on their handling and enforcement of hygiene measures
Handling of special opening hours for risk groups	Customers that belong to a risk group can quickly check whether the store offers special opening hours for certain risk groups
Offer customer tracking without entry control sensor	Track customers via WiFi signals (or similar signaling technology) during they visit the store to enable a system that does not rely on an entry control sensor
Data privacy and protection	Improve data privacy and protection particularly if customer tracking is involved

the employees. A bad rating would certainly tempt the owners to take action. One of the interviewees pointed out that it might be useful if users could indicate in the application that they belong to a risk group. It would be useful to have it at a glance which supermarkets offer special opening hours for risk groups.

Another interviewee mentioned that in the future it might be possible to develop to the extent that the application is functional even without the use of the Connfair Entry system light. The interviewee suggested that not all shops would be able to buy the traffic light service, especially very small shops. Without the dependency on Connfair the PlanYourShoppingSafe application could be offered to a broader range of shops. In order to realize this, further research in the area of tracking can be done by using Wi-Fi signal data.

One interviewee was concerned about data protection and privacy. The interviewee was worried that his visits could be traced by third parties. To get many users to use the application, data protection and privacy would have to be guaranteed. For this it would be important that the data is secured against unauthorized access and no personal data is collected without permission. Possible solutions could involve encrypted data stores and anonymized data records.

Conclusion

This paper developed a new concept for better management of hygiene measures currently in place in the retail sector to combat the pandemic. Furthermore, it was analyzed which problems have not yet been resolved despite hygiene measures and their effects the shopping experience of customers. During literature research on this topic and the interviews conducted, two problems were frequently mentioned, namely, crowds in the supermarket and long queues in front of shops.

In order to develop a solution to overcome these issues, a concept was developed that extends current traffic light technology. The Customer Flow Control System offers stores the possibility to use sensors to fully monitor and control the current customer workload in the store. The reactions to the prototype concept were consistently positive. The interviewees were very interested in the solution that addresses the problem of crowded shops and long queues and confirmed that they would use it. They think that it would be worthwhile to implement such an application and that it would meet great approval. The interviews also revealed topics for further development. In summary, the application offers a promising approach to support people in their daily tasks, shopping, during the pandemic and make it more comfortable.

Overall, based on literature research and the conducted interview study, the developed prototype concept indicates that usage of digital technology can decrease infectious risk for employees and customers while at the same time improve the shopping experience.

References

Aylott, & Mitchell. (1998). An exploratory study of grocery shopping stressors. *International Journal of Retail & Distribution Management, 26*, 362–373. https://doi.org/10.1108/09590559810237908.

Bakibinga-Gaswaga, E., Bakibinga, S., Bakibinga, D. B. M., & Bakibinga, P. (2020). Digital technologies in the COVID-19 responses in sub-Saharan Africa: Policies, problems and promises. *The Pan African Medical Journal, 35*(38).

Beck, & Hensher. (2020). *Insights into the impact of COVID-19 on household travel, working, activities and shopping in Australia – the early days under restrictions*. Institute of Transport and Logistic Studies (ITLS), The University of Sydney Business School, Sydney.

BGWH. (2020). Wie viele Kunden sollten höchstens gleichzeitig in einem Markt oder in einer Verkaufsstelle anwesend sein? Retrieved June 22, 2020, from https://www.bghw.de/die-bghw/faq/faqs-rund-um-corona/spezielle-fragen-fuer-beschaeftigte-im-handel-und-in-der-warenlogistik/wie-viele-kunden-sollten-hoechstens-gleichzeitig-in-einem-markt-oder-in-einer-verkaufsstelle-anwesend-sein

Connfair. (2020). *Einlassampel*. Retrieved June 11, 2020, from https://einlass-ampel.de/#tve-jump-17270cf9c54

Conrad. (1994). A real-time people counter Tricor Systems Inc. Richard Johnsonbaugh DePaul University. ACM 089791-6,4.7,-6/94/000.

Desai. (2020). Food safety and COVID-19: COVID-19 is an infectious disease caused by the novel coronavirus SARS-CoV-2. *JAMA, 323*(19).

Ebster, C., & Garaus, M. (2011). *Store design and visual merchandising: Creating store space that encourages buying*. New York: Business Expert Press.

Fletcher, & Griffith. (2020). Digital transformation during a lockdown. *International Journal of Information Management*. Salford Business School, University of Salford, Maxwell building the crescent, Salford M5 4WT, UK.

Garcia, et al. (2013). Directional people counter based on head tracking. *IEEE Transactions on Industrial Electronics, 60*(9). https://doi.org/10.1109/TIE.2012.2206330

Grashuis, Skevas, & Segoviaa. (2020). Grocery shopping preferences during the COVID-19 Pandemic. *Sustainability, 12*, 5369. https://doi.org/10.3390/su12135369

Güsken, S. R., Janssen, D., & Hees, F. (2019). Online grocery platforms—Understanding consumer acceptance. In *Proceedings of the 2019 ISPIM Connects Conference*. International Society for Professional Innovation Management, Manchester. Retrieved from https://www.ispim-innovation.com/

Jayaweera, et al. (2020). Transmission of COVID-19 virus by droplets and aerosols: A critical review on the unresolved dichotomy. *Elsevier Public Health Emergency Collection*. https://doi.org/10.1016/j.envres.2020.109819

Köhler, & Klett. (2016). *Neue Rechtsprechung zur Berechnung der Verkaufsfläche eines Einzelhandelsbetriebe*. Retrieved July 10, 2020, from https://koehler-klett.de/newsletter/juni-2016/neue-rechtsprechung-zur-berechnung-der-verkaufsflache-eines-einzelhandelsbetriebes

Li, et al. (2015). Wi-Counter: Smartphone-based people counter using crowdsourced Wi-Fi signal data. *IEEE Transactions on Human-Machine Systems, 45*(4), 442–452.

Lobach. (2020) Living in a worldwide quarantine: A social practice theory analysis of the grocery shopping change during COVID-19 crisis.

Mukhopadhyay, B. (2020). Effectively managing remote workplace during COVID-19. *The Sentinel, Post Editorial*, 19th March.

Munbodth, E. (2020). Coronavirus: 20,000 high street shops that have closed during lockdown will never reopen. *The Mirror*, 26th March 2020. Retrieved July 08, 2020, from https://www.mirror.co.uk/money/coronavirus-more-20000-shops-closed-21756815

Nicola, et al. (2020). The socio-economic implications of the coronavirus pandemic (COVID-19): A review. *Elsevier Public Health Emergency Collection*. https://doi.org/10.1016/j.ijsu.2020.04.018

Nielsen. (1993). *Usability engineering*. Morgan Kaufmann Publishers Inc. https://doi.org/10.5555/529793.

Pasco, et al. (2020). *COVID-19 in Austin, Texas: Epidemiological assessment of grocery shopping*. The University of Texas at Austin COVID-19 Modeling Consortium.

Reimers, et al. (2020). *Supporting the continuation of teaching and learning during the COVID-19 pandemic annotated resources for online learning*. Retrieved July 09, 2020, from http://www.oecd.org/education/Supporting-the-continuation-of-teaching-and-learning-during-the-COVID-19-pandemic.pdf

RKI. (2020). *Epidomologie*. Retrieved July 04, 2020, from https://www.rki.de/SharedDocs/FAQ/NCOV2019/FAQ_Liste_Epidemiologie.html

Sudrajat. (2020). *Changes in organizational structure and service system in supermarkets when pandemic COVID-19 digital business*. Faculty of Economics and Business Padjadjaran University.

Whitelaw, et al. (2020). Applications of digital technology in COVID-19 pandemic planning and response. https://doi.org/10.1016/S2589-7500(20)30142-4

WHO. (2020) *WHO timeline – COVID-19*. Retrieved July 07, 2020, from https://www.who.int/news-room/detail/08-04-2020-who- timeline%2D%2D-covid-19

Chapter 10
Developing a Concept for a Digital Restaurant System to Minimize Risk of Infection for Customers and Personnel

Sefa Basar

Abstract The COVID-19 pandemic changed both the daily life of people and the daily processes of companies. Virtually all business sectors had to accept new governmental regulations and restrictions. One of the most affected industries is the gastronomy sector, where interpersonal contact seems unavoidable. As a result, digitized solutions must be introduced into this sector in order to keep the business running during a pandemic. An optimal solution would be to perform an ordering process in restaurants without any human interaction. This could be achieved by using a voice-controlled terminal device that includes an intelligent voice assistant like "Alexa" from Amazon. The introduction of such a solution is developed in this paper. Advantages such as contactless ordering could revolutionize the whole industry. The material used for this study consists mainly of scientific research papers in the field of information systems and innovative technologies.

Keywords Digital restaurant system · Contactless ordering · Gastronomy · Virtual assistant · Voice service platform

Introduction

The COVID-19 pandemic changed the daily life and business around the world. Virtually all business sectors had to accept new regulations and restrictions from the government in the recent months. In the worst case, this even led to the closure of many companies. Above all, sectors relying on face-to-face service for their customers have been hit hardest by this pandemic since social interaction and work is the most important value-adding activity in these sectors. One of these sectors is the catering industry. As the catering industry in particular is dependent on daily operations, many restaurants unfortunately had to close due to insolvency

S. Basar (✉)
University of Cologne, Cologne, Germany
e-mail: sbasar@smail.uni-koeln.de

C. Hovestadt et al. (eds.), *Digital Responses to Covid-19*, SpringerBriefs in Information Systems, https://doi.org/10.1007/978-3-030-66611-8_10

(Faulenbach 2020). Some restaurants were able to avoid insolvency during this time by offering a delivery service (e.g., through a web shop). The situation forced many restaurants to take first steps toward digitalization (Gies 2020). Health experts predict that the pandemic will continue and there could be a second wave of COVID-19 spread during Winter 2020 (Robert Koch Institute 2020a, b).

Problematic is the high infection rate compared to other diseases and asymptomatic course of disease that makes it difficult to track infected people. In the gastronomy sector, the infection risk is high because service personnel of the restaurants have contact with many customers (Robert Koch Institute 2020a, b).

Although the government has been trying to prevent an economic shock through a variety of aid packages (Bundesfinanzministerium 2020), and has already weakened some hygiene regulations, many operators have not been able to avoid the shutdown of their businesses. Even larger restaurant chains such as Vapiano could not survive for long (Focus 2020).

As mentioned before, most of the restaurants were shut due to the COVID-19 pandemic lockdown regulations by the government. In general, restaurants are generally organized via direct interaction between customers, waiters, and kitchen personnel for placing orders, paying, and serving dishes. To decrease risk of infections, a contactless ordering and payment system is necessary.

At the same time, restaurants face specific challenges that threaten their quality of service such as waiting times, employee thefts and burglary, and preparation and serving food. Therefore, the aim of this paper is to answer the following research question:

> How is it possible to establish a contactless ordering process for restaurants in order to minimize the risk of infection of customers and waitresses, while maintaining the same quality of service?

We develop a solution concept for a digital restaurant system that can minimize risk of infection for customers and restaurant personnel. We discuss benefits and challenges of our proposed solution and provide an outlook.

Related Work

Service Challenges of Restaurants

The main challenge that restaurants or Cafés have is to satisfy the needs of their customers and to meet customer satisfaction. Restaurants face specific challenges that threaten their quality of service such as waiting times, employee thefts and burglary, and preparation and serving food. We will discuss each of these in the following.

Apart from the quality of the served food and meal, the customers require a convenient way to order and pay their foods, as they get frustrated if they wait too long for ordering or paying. Restaurants might lose customers consequently if they are not satisfied (Ahsan et al. 2014). Most of the customers chose to avoid restaurants based on bad experience, which results in low revenues (Davis et al. 2016).

A customer spends in average about 15 min waiting in a restaurant (Vries et al. 2018). Researchers indicate that without waiting a restaurant might increase the total revenues by nearly 15% (Vries et al. 2018). According to research, 58% of customers would be willing to spend more if their waiting times were cut in half (Oracle Food & Beverage 2019).

Furthermore, customers are eager to use new technology that would improve their food experience since 68% of surveyed customers in a study indicated that they are interested to use a mobile application to order food and drink (Oracle Food & Beverage 2019). Waiting times also result in more time spent at a table, which means that a table is occupied for a longer time. The restaurants tend to serve as many customers as possible and thus try to avoid long occupied tables. Summarizing, customers' waiting times is one problem for restaurants that negatively affects customer satisfaction and the total revenues of restaurants.

Apart from waitressing and serving customers, there is the problem of cash thefts in restaurants, either due to employee theft or simply burglary. The number of revenue loss due to employee theft totals between three and 6 billion US Dollars annually and contributes to about 50% of small business failures within the first year (Holmes 2011).

Generally, cooks prepare food according to order notes provided by the waiters. Dealing with paper notes can lead to confusion when multiple orders are processed by the cooks. They lose track of the orders, sometimes prepare the wrong food, and even miss to prepare food. Digital tools help to visualize orders and provide systematic overviews of orders. This is currently missing in many restaurants. The same accounts for waiters because they often get confused with paper notes such that the wrong food is noted or served to the tables.

The State of Digitalization in Restaurants

The restaurant industry is a relatively non-digitalized industry that relies on physical contact. Except for the possibility of ordering food online through intermediary providers such as Lieferando or an own web shop, hardly any digitized solutions have been introduced in broader terms. Although approaches are available for digitization of singular increments of the ordering process in restaurants, an entirely digitized process concept from ordering to payment does not exist.

One widely discussed approach is ordering on terminals with a touch screen (Schader 2017). Here, the customer orders his food by selecting it on a touch screen and paying by card. However, there is a risk of infection by touching the display, which could spread infections. The survival time of the Corona virus varies depending on the material of the surface. Since displays consist of a layer of glass and plastic, experts estimate that viruses can survive for up to 72 h on these surfaces (Robert Koch Institute 2020a, b). Another approach is to place the order via the customer's mobile device (Tanpure et al. 2013). The customer is able to browse and select items from the menu via on his own device to reduce contact with foreign objects. Mobile payments have been researched in the context of online ordering processes via mobile phone. Basically, the customer has the option of paying for the order via mobile phone, but is served in the restaurant (Gatronovi 2020).

Although voice-based automated dialogue systems for restaurant orders have been envisioned and prototyped early on (López-Cózar et al. 1997), we do not see their dissemination into the restaurant business. Many speech-based natural user interfaces have increased in capacity in the recent years (López et al. 2017).

A New Concept for a Digital Restaurant System

To develop a new digital restaurant system concept, the base assumption is that an optimal solution would be performing the ordering process without any human interaction. On the basis of this assumption, in the following, we develop a concept for a voice-controlled terminal device that includes an intelligent voice assistant. Our concept is based on the Echo Dot device from Amazon including the voice assistant "Alexa". Since the use of autonomous "IoT" (Internet of Things) devices such as the Echo Dot continues to grow and become more efficient (Göbel 2019), the trend is towards more and more IoT devices being used in everyday life is real (Brandt 2019). Thus, we argue that the widely spread Echo Dot that many customers are familiar with provides a useful platform basis.

Overview of the Digital Restaurant System

The voice-controlled Alexa system could bring digitization to restaurants and Cafés. The system could be used at each table of the restaurant. It would be integrated with a digital screen that displays the menu card. The system could be used to digitize the ordering and paying process in a restaurant. It would work as a such called "Self-Service Kiosk" where customers can place their orders while speaking to Alexa and where customers can pay directly via digital payment services (e.g., PayPal). The order can be transmitted to the kitchen after receiving the payment and would be displayed on a web application to the cooks. They would prepare the food and set the order to "Done" in the web application. Alexa could give notification to the customers that the order is ready and then the customers could pick up the food themselves at a counter. This system allows contactless ordering and paying. Restaurants can create a low-infection-risk environment where customers do not directly interact with waiters and cooks. These restaurants could be able to prevent a total shut down while adhering to strict hygiene regulations.

The System provides various functionalities for the customer. Figure 10.1 depicts a use case diagram of the system solution.

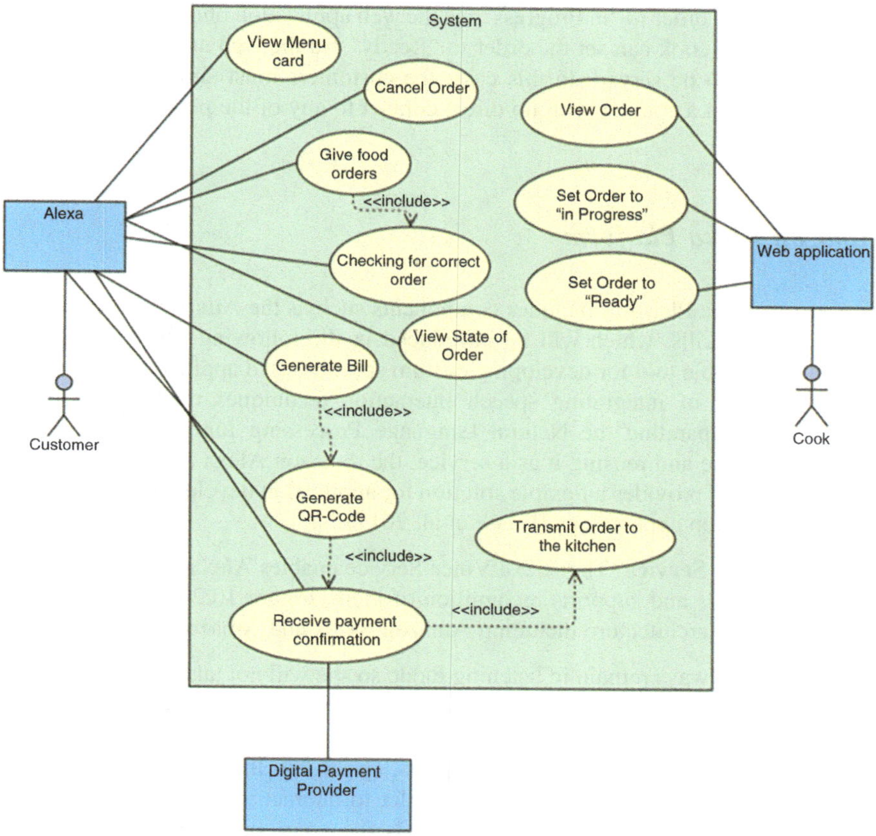

Fig. 10.1 Use case model for the digital restaurant system

The system shows the customers the menu card in the integrated Alexa screen. When the customer is ready for ordering, the system takes orders via Alexa. After the order is placed, the system verifies the correct items in the order by repeating and displaying the order. The customer rechecks the order and confirms or changes it. The system generates the bill and simultaneously generates a QR-Code, which contains a link to the digital payment provider. The customer scans the QR-Code by his mobile device and is directed to the digital payment provider. After paying the bill, the system will receive a confirmation of successful payment and will display the confirmation to the users. Along with that, the order will be transmitted to the kitchen. In advance of paying the bill, the user can cancel the order any time by speaking to Alexa. The order cannot be cancelled after receiving the payment confirmation. The user can review the state of his order at any time, after the payment is received. A web application displays the received orders by listing each item and quantity. Each order contains the table number as an additional information. The cook can set the order to "in Progress" via the web application once meal preparation has begun. The cook can set the order to "Ready" via the web application once the food is ready to be served. In this case, the customers must simply pick up their prepared food at a counter with no direct contact to any of the personnel.

Amazon Alexa Platform

Amazon's Alexa Platform includes components such as the Amazon Voice Service and Amazon Skills, which will be introduced in the following. The platform has become a valuable tool for developing custom speech-based applications. However, the complexity of integrating speech interaction techniques made development difficult. By separating the Natural Language Processing functionality from the application logic and reusing it as a service, the Amazon Alexa Software Development Kit (SDK) provides a flexible solution for application developers to implement their voice-driven applications (Haase et al. 2017).

Amazon Voice Service The Alexa Voice Service enables Alexa devices to receive voice commands and supports recognition of them. Figure 10.2 provides an overview of overall architecture including Amazon Skills and Amazon Voice Services.

Alexa will always remain in listening mode so she will not take voice commands until the word "Alexa" wakes her up. Each time Alexa wakes up, she only takes one voice command and then returns to listening mode (Lei et al. 2018).

As shown in Fig. 10.2, the user must first speak into the echo device or into a third-party device that supports Alexa in order to interact with Alexa. The speaker then records the user's voice data and sends the voice input to the Alexa voice service. Once the Alexa voice service receives the voice data, it analyzes the voice input and transforms it into a JSON format for further use. It then sends the data to the Alexa Skill Kit interface, where it decides which function the user wants to interact with. It then sends the JSON data to the HTTP endpoint running the server code and executes the appropriate function. The HTTP endpoint can either be the Amazon Lambda server offered by Amazon or another HTTP server. At this point, it can interact with other third-party REST APIs to retrieve and process additional necessary information. Once the server has completed the execution of the request, it sends the JSON output data back to the Alexa Web Service where the Alexa voice service processes the text into voice data. It then sends the Alexa voice recording to the speaker device so that the user can hear Alexa's response (Leong 2018).

Alexa Skills Alexa Skills are voice-driven functions that developers can create for the cloud-based Alexa service that support Amazon devices (Alhadlaq et al. 2017). A skill is required for processing the user's voice messages and transforming them into specific service requests with provided parameters. Each skill can define a series of service requests that are called intents (Haase et al. 2017). To expand the platform, Amazon enables development of third-party applications, so-called "skills", which

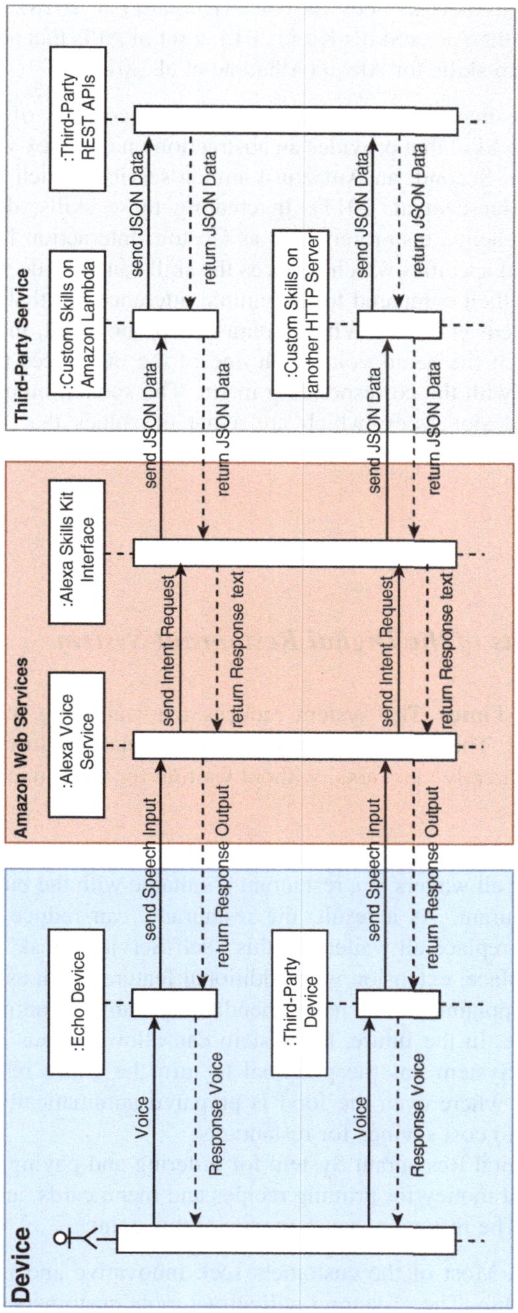

Fig. 10.2 Architecture of Amazon skills and Amazon voice services (Leong 2018, p. 2)

use Alexa voice services. Many companies are actively developing Alexa Skills to provide easy access to their services via voice (Kumar et al. 2018). For this reason, Amazon introduced the Alexa Skills Kit in 2015, a set of APIs that allow developers to create voice-driven skills for Alexa (Alhadlaq et al. 2017).

The Alexa voice interaction mechanism generally consists of two functional parts. First, an Alexa Skill that provides an abstraction on complex voice processing and service creation. Second, an Amazon Lambda service, which implements the application logic (Haase et al. 2017). In creating these skills, developers must provide the intent schema, also referred to as Custom Interaction Model, which is a JSON structure that specifies which services the skill can provide when it receives voice input. This is then compared to the sample utterances so that the system can recognize which intent is called. When a phrase is pronounced, the Alexa service will attempt to match the heard voice with one of the utterances and execute the function associated with the corresponding intent. The spoken input data may also include user-defined slot types, which are a list of values that are assigned to specific tags.

Discussion

Expected Benefits of the Digital Restaurant System

Reduced Waiting Times The system reduces the wait time of customers for ordering and paying. The "Self-Service Kiosk" functionality allows the customers to order their food directly via Alexa, without waiting for a menu card or the waiter to take the orders.

Cost Savings The system takes over the main tasks of a waiter. The system can be used to even replace all waiters in a restaurant if suitable with the business model of the respective restaurant. As a result, the restaurants can reduce the number of waiters or can even replace all waiters by this "Self-Service Kiosk". Once a digital infrastructure is in place, extension with additional features such as online reservations, customer complaints, food recommendations, table cleaning and location guiding is realizable. In the future, the system can allow various digital payment opportunities. The System has the potential to turn the entire restaurant into an automated business where even the food is prepared automatically. Reduction in personnel will lead to cost savings for restaurants.

By using the Digital Restaurant System for ordering and paying, the restaurants do not have to spend money for printing recipes and menu cards, and also no order notes are required. The restaurant saves money at this point.

Digital Innovation Most of the customers seek innovative and modern ways to improve their daily life. The restaurant will attract more customers by applying the Digital Restaurant System, as it uses the most innovative features for ordering and paying. Customers may conceive restaurants with the Digital Restaurant System in place as innovative and appealing.

No Cash Money and Safety for Owner The Digital Restaurant System allows the customers to digitally pay. Hence, no cash money is needed or processed in a restaurant. This reduces the risk for employee theft and burglary. Employees would not be able to steal cash money and burglars would have no profit in breaking into a restaurant. As a result, the restaurant would be safer and would increase its revenues by avoiding these risks.

Expected Challenges

Apart from the benefits mentioned above, the system would pose some challenges to restaurants. The first and most important issue would be the acoustic recognition of the commands of the Alexa device in case of high levels of noise within the restaurants. It is still the case that the end devices have problems interpreting the commands correctly when overlapping with noise such as other voices speaking simultaneously. In this case it could be perhaps possible to use an external and directed microphone. The next point would be the willingness of the restaurant owners to switch to a digital infrastructure that is not yet really established anywhere in Germany. In case of adoption, waiters would be directly affected and might lose their jobs. The digital payment system would limit the customer segment to adults as minors are not yet eligible for some payment methods. On the other hand, older seniors who are not familiar with digital devices may have problems placing orders. A change in the system would therefore be an intervention in the classic "restaurant culture".

Discussion

The COVID-19 pandemic forces organizations in many sectors to take further steps towards digitalization. In the long term, this situation does not necessarily have to be a loss-making step because it may enable them to develop better or even completely new services. Had this transition to digital systems taken place earlier, many owners may have even saved their businesses from closing down or going bankrupt. Thus, many sectors could voluntarily embark on the digital revolution in the future. In a sector with low digitization such as gastronomy, the voice-controlled order system could have saved many restaurants from insolvency. Furthermore, the system could have been extended and adapted to other sectors where social contact with many people is also essential (such as the hotel industry).

References

Ahsan, M., Islam, R., & Alam, A. (2014). Study of queuing system of a busy restaurant and a proposed facilitate queuing system. *IOSR Journal of Mechanical and Civil Engineering*, 31.

Alhadlaq, A., Tang, J., & Almaymoni, M. (2017). Privacy in the Amazon Alexa skills ecosystem. In *17th privacy enhancing technologies symposium* (pp. 1–2).

Bundesfinanzministerium. (2020, May 22). *Das Kon-junk-tur-pro-gramm*. https://www.bundesfinanzministerium.de/Content/DE/Standardartikel/Themen/Schlaglichter/Konjunkturpaket/2020-06-03-konjunkturpaket-beschlossen.html

Davis, R., Rogers, T., & Huang, Y. (2016). A survey of recent developments in queue wait time forecasting methods. *International Conference Foundations of Computer Science*, 84.

De Vries, J., Roy, D., & De Koster, R. (2018). Worth the wait? How restaurant waiting time influences customer behavior and revenue. *Journal of Operations Management*.

Focus. (2020, March 24). *Dramatischer Umsatzeinbruch: Folgen der Ladenschließungen: Restaurantkette Vapiano ist zahlungsunfähig*. https://www.focus.de/finanzen/boerse/angeordnete-lokalschliessungen-restaurantkette-vapiano-ist-zahlungsunfaehig_id_11793661.html

Gatronovi. (2020). https://www.gastronovi.com/de/module/bestellsystem/

Haase, P., Nikolov, A. N., Tram, J., Kozlov, A., & Herzig, D. M. (2017). *Alexa, ask Wikidata! Voice interaction with knowledge graphs using Amazon Alexa*. International Semantic Web Conference.

Holmes, H. (2011). *Employee theft in restaurants: Perceptions about theft-related activities and reporting behaviors* (p. 1).

Kai Gies. (2020, March 31). *Auch kleine Berliner Geschäfte setzen auf Lieferservice*. https://www.tagesspiegel.de/berlin/in-der-COVID-19virus-krise-sind-webshops-gefragt-auch-kleine-berliner-geschaefte-setzen-auf-lieferservice/25694422.html [10.07.2020]

Kumar, D., Paccagnella, R., Murley, P., Hennenfent, E., Mason, J., & Bates, A. (2018). Skill squatting attacks on Amazon Alexa. In *27th security symposium security* (18. Aufl., pp. 33–47) Baltimore: USENIX Association.

Lars Faulenbach. (2020, July 10). *Restaurants, Kneipen und Cafés in NRW droht die Pleite*. Retrieved from https://www1.wdr.de/nachrichten/themen/COVID-19virus/gastwirte-COVID-19krise106.html)

Lei, X., Tu, G.-H., Liu, A. X., Kamran, A., Li, C.-Y., & Xie, T. (2018). The insecurity of home digital voice assistants – Amazon Alexa as a case study. *Clinical Orthopaedics and Related Research, 1*.

Leong, R. (2018). *Analyzing the privacy attack landscape for Amazon Alexa devices* (p. 2).

López, G., Quesada, L., & Guerrero, L. A. (2017, July). Alexa vs. Siri vs. Cortana vs. Google Assistant: A comparison of speech-based natural user interfaces. In *International conference on applied human factors and ergonomics* (pp. 241–250). Cham: Springer.

López-Cózar, R., García, P., Diaz-Verdejo, J., & Rubio, A. J. (1997). *A voice activated dialogue system for fast-food restaurant applications*. Fifth European Conference on Speech Communication and Technology.

Markus Oliver Göbel. (2019). *Immer mehr IoT Projekte in Unternehmen*. Retrieved from https://www.basecamp.digital/internet-of-things-studie-2019-immer-mehr-iot-projekte-in-unternehmen/

Mathias Brandt. (2019). *Wie groß sind die "Next Big Things" tatsächlich?* Retrieved from https://de.statista.com/infografik/16558/geschaetzte-einnahmen-aus-dem-verkauf-von-tech-produkten-in-den-usa/

Oracle Food & Beverage. (2019, May 09). *Are you ready for the stadium of the future?* Retrieved from https://blogs.oracle.com/foodandbeverage/future-of-stadium-point-of-sale-1

Peer Schader. (2017, November 13). *Antippen statt anstellen: Wie Vapiano und McDonald's den Bestellprozess im Schnellrestaurant umkrempeln*. Retrieved from https://www.supermarktblog.

com/2017/11/13/antippen-statt-anstellen-wie-vapiano-und-mcdonalds-den-bestellprozess-im-schnellrestaurant-umkrempeln/

Robert Koch Institute. (2020a, July 10). *SARS-CoV-2 Steckbrief zur COVID-19virus-Krankheit-2019 (COVID-19)*. Retrieved from https://www.rki.de/DE/Content/InfAZ/N/Neuartiges_COVID-19virus/Steckbrief.html#doc13776792bodyText11

Robert Koch Institute. (2020b, July 2). *Epidemiologie: Antworten auf häufig gestellte Fragen zum COVID-19virus SARS-CoV-2/Krankheit COVID-19*. Retrieved from https://www.rki.de/SharedDocs/FAQ/NCOV2019/gesamt.htm

Tanpure, S. S., Shidankar, P. R., & Joshi, M. M. (2013). Automated food ordering system with real-time customer feedback. *International Journal of Advanced Research in Computer Science and Software Engineering, 3*(2).

Chapter 11
Toward a New Wave of Digital Responses to COVID-19

Christian Hovestadt, Jan Recker, Janek Richter, and Karl Werder

Abstract The essays in this book help understanding how digitally enabled responses to the COVID-19 pandemic can be developed through digital innovation, digital transformation, and digital entrepreneurship. Based on the nine essays, we suggest three important future research areas in which information systems scholars should make active contributions in the ongoing fight against the pandemic: the surveillance society, the misconception of digital solutions, and the design of practical solutions. In addition, we highlight new challenges for research and practice that arise from the ongoing pandemic.

Keywords COVID-19 pandemic · Digitally enabled response · Surveillance society · Digital solution · Practical solution design

Summary of Contributions in This Book

The collection of nine student essays that form the main body of this book presents an overview over how information systems (IS) research may be drawn upon to contribute to the global fight against the COVID-19 pandemic. Collectively, the essays demonstrate how the disruptive and uncertain changes to the societal and economic environment that a global pandemic triggers can lead to new digital innovations emerging, transformational processes being catalyzed, and entrepreneurial ventures adapting and pivoting. The new ideas and changes were not born free, they were externally enabled (Davidsson et al. 2020), by force if you will. But this does not mean that the emerging innovations, transformations, and ventures are qualitatively worse than the solutions they replace, nor are they temporary placeholders in the search for a return to the "old reality". Instead, COVID-19 enabled digital innovation, transformation, and entrepreneurship, and it launched and

C. Hovestadt · J. Recker (✉) · J. Richter · K. Werder
University of Cologne, Cologne, Germany
e-mail: hovestadt@wiso.uni-koeln.de; jan.recker@wiso.uni-koeln.de; janek.richter@wiso.uni-koeln.de; werder@wiso.uni-koeln.de

C. Hovestadt et al. (eds.), *Digital Responses to Covid-19*, SpringerBriefs in Information Systems, https://doi.org/10.1007/978-3-030-66611-8_11

accelerated the transition to what will be our new reality (Hitt et al. 2021), our adaptation to a "new normal" (Mithani 2020).

The nine student essays sketch out how such adaptations can be digitally enabled. In Chap. 2, Fritz Hädrich compared different implementations of COVID-19 tracking dashboards and investigated their role in informing the public during a global pandemic. For his case study, the author selected three popular dashboards with different characteristics: one with only local data of a single country, one that focused on a single country but also had global data, and one that had a global target audience. The author explored the dashboards in light of criteria stipulated by representation theory (Burton-Jones et al. 2017; Wand and Weber 1990; Weber 1997). He found that the dashboards complied well with the mapping condition, that is, every state of the real world maps to at least one state in the IS. The dashboards adhered to the state-tracking criterion to a medium extent, that is, changes in the course of the pandemic can only be reconstructed in a limited way. However, none the dashboards considered the external event condition, that is, distinct real-world events are shown that may influence the course of the pandemic. In consequence, the dashboards also failed regarding the sequencing condition, which would require that the dashboards put external events into a temporally and logically coherent order. In conclusion, the author investigated a distinct digital innovation that is unique to the pandemic. He discussed multiple implementations of this innovation on an individual level and developed empirical knowledge in form of a case study.

In Chap. 3, Laurenz Kriehn reconstructed the process of how the German COVID-19 contact tracing app was developed. In the chapter, general requirements for contact tracing apps were derived, which other countries can review for their implementations. Afterwards, the specific case of the development of the German contact tracing app was discussed with a focus on its transition from a centralized to a decentralized architecture. He described the entire development process originating from initial idea at the start of the pandemic in Germany until the deployment of the app and showed how the process was shaped by public discussions and expert opinions. Finally, it was determined that the German application addressed most of the initially determined privacy concerns, although it did not prevent some high-effort small-scale surveillance approaches. In conclusion, the author discussed a digital innovation that was a direct consequence of the pandemic. Although the chapter focused on an individual contact tracing app, the level of analysis was maintained at the societal level, as the investigated contact tracing app was commissioned for an entire country. Empirical knowledge was derived in form of a case study, which other countries can review for their implementations of contact tracing apps.

In Chap. 4, Ivan Trilevic addressed the problem that children's education may suffer from a lockdown during a pandemic. He developed a new concept for a digital platform that brings together children and providers of online educational courses. He found that the main problem for parents are lock-in effects into specific courses where children might lose interest quickly, while course providers face much administrative effort, especially for registration and deregistration of their participants. The proposed platform solves this by offering flexible membership models while relieving course providers from managing registration and payment processes. In conclusion, this chapter explored a digital innovation on an organization level, using a fictional platform provider as level of analysis. The developed knowledge is design-oriented as it provides guidelines for how a platform for children's education courses should be designed.

In Chap. 5, Simon Friedrich Murillo investigated the role of digital tools for digital natives and their role in support of learning during the global pandemic. During the first few months of the pandemic in Germany, schools were closed, requiring students to develop a structure and process for independent learning at home. They had to conduct their own learning activities and find ways to provide a structured and effective learning environment in the absence of school visits and classroom activities. Disparities in socially and technically possible developments of such a learning environment at home lead to diverse learning experience and outcomes during the lockdown for individual students. Students that grew up in technology-savvy households were better equipped than students in households where the use of technology was limited, especially when parents were only able to offer limited after-school support. The author suggested that virtual schools can help close the learning gap and provide equal opportunities for all students. An increasing adoption of virtual schools could educate both, teachers and students, in using digital tools for their teaching and learning activities. With these skills, students and teachers alike would be better equipped to handle the transition from a physical to a digital classroom, something that overwhelmed teachers and students during this pandemic. In addition, the author suggested the importance of these digital skills that students need in order to succeed in their future academic or business environment. In conclusion, the author explored the digital transformation of individuals, deriving conceptual and design-oriented knowledge.

In Chap. 6, Jana Feldkamp investigated the rise of the social media platform *TikTok* during the global pandemic. During global efforts to fight the pandemic, physical distancing guidelines were enforced. Yet, individuals still sought social connections with each other. Since individuals were not able to connect and recognize each other physically, they utilized social media platforms such as TikTok in even more intensive ways for this purpose. The author identified three success factors that helped the TikTok platform to rise to new heights during the pandemic: a hyper-personalized algorithm based on artificial intelligence, an open approach where everybody could use the platform without registration, and the migration of influencers to TikTok, which lead to an increase in both content and users. Looking forward, the platform is threatened to be banned by certain countries. In response, it seeks to establish itself as both a marketing platform and a learning platform, attempting to provide value to its users and generate revenue from its large userbase. In conclusion, the chapter explored the digital transformation of an entire ecosystem, deriving conceptual knowledge from a case study.

In Chap. 7, Zacharias Schrage investigated the control practices used by software development teams during the global pandemic. Software development teams faced the same constraints through physical distancing as the rest of the society; however, the demand in software applications, especially for collaboration software such as

Zoom, Jive, or Microsoft Teams, received a surge in demand. Hence, while many things were uncertain and in flux, management still needed to assure that software improvements and updates were delivered with quality and speed. The author reviewed typical control practices in software development, their applicability to agile and traditional software development, and how they could possibly be adapted during the COVID-19 pandemic. For example, he suggested how daily scrums could be enacted remotely using video conferencing services and digital progress trackers, or how formal communication plans could be enacted through messenger services such as Slack on the basis of defined system access privileges. Overall, the study suggested that many control practices are still usable despite the pandemic. While some practices required adaptation, only few control practices were no longer applicable. In conclusion, the chapter explored digital transformation within organizations, deriving conceptual knowledge.

In Chap. 8, Jana Teutenberg investigated how a new digital venture identified digital opportunities in the COVID-19 pandemic to transform their existing business model. The event business market had been struck by the pandemic as large parts of the event-based cultural life came to a halt because of physical distancing guidelines. The author focused on the case of a new venture operating exactly in the outdoor event market. The new venture traditionally offered information about little-known cultural events and locations in urban life. During the pandemic, they decided to re-orient their digital platform capabilities to pivot from a "going-out concept" to a "stay-inside concept", which established fit with physical distancing measures. The venture successfully and quickly adapted to the new situation and offered customers as well as artists a new digital platform where events could take place in a digital format, for example, via video streaming from an artist's home. The digital platform also enabled fans to support artists with micropayments and establish a sense of community through several ways of interaction. Multiple strategy recommendations for new ventures were developed by the author to learn from this case example. In conclusion, the chapter explored digital transformation through a case study analysis.

In Chap. 9, Shanice Casado Gracia developed an application concept for managing hygiene measures in the grocery retail sector. The retail sector had been particularly struck by the governmental legislation enforcing the implementation of hygiene measures for customers in supermarkets and grocery stores. At the same time, stores had been under strain through customer peaks for essential groceries. The author developed a practical digital solution relying on already-available technology for customer flow management. The available solutions were reviewed, and the author proposed new feature extensions for integration into the application architecture. The new solution's features were evaluated by interviewing potential users. An important learning was that new digital solutions during the pandemic had to effectively address hygiene measures while at the same time remaining fit for daily use. Otherwise, they would not be viable in the long-term. In conclusion, the chapter addressed the designing of a new concept for digital transformation suitable for the grocery retail sector.

In Chap. 10, Sefa Basar developed a concept for a digital restaurant system that minimizes risk of infection for customers and personnel. The restaurant industry is a rather non-digital industry that relies on physical contact. While the restaurant industry had seen several concepts for digitalization, the implementation of advanced digital solutions for entire processes had not advanced even though digital solutions could reduce risks of infections because of a lack of need for physical interactions, for example, during ordering. The developed concept for a digital restaurant builds on the idea of using voice-based automated dialogue systems for customer interaction. The Amazon Alexa platform and associated skills were presented as a foundation for such a system that would be extendable via new skills. While taking note of challenges of such a system, the author discussed expected benefits as well, such as reduced waiting times, cost savings for the operator, digital innovativeness, and safety for owner. In conclusion, the chapter designed a new concept for digital transformation suitable for the restaurant sector.

Future Research Opportunities

This book presented nine essays for three types of digitally enabled responses to COVID-19: digital innovation, digital transformation, and digital entrepreneurship. Across the nine essays, different levels of analysis (individual, organization, ecosystem) were investigated, and different types of knowledge contributions were provided (empirical, conceptual, design-oriented). Together, the essays provide an overview of digital responses across different levels and forms of business. They also provide a glimpse of how digitally enabled responses to COVID-19 might become efficacious solutions. Yet of course, the pandemic affects all aspects of private and professional live, so nine essays cannot possibly be a comprehensive coverage of all potential solutions enabled by digital technologies, nor of the entire problem space that would benefit from digitally enabled responses. In looking forward, we now identify two central avenues for future IS research contributions. First, more conceptual work is needed on digital innovation. Second, more empirical work is needed in regard to digital transformation and entrepreneurship.

In this book, the three essays on digital innovation focus on empirical and design-oriented research. Digital innovation are novel product or service offerings that are enabled by or embodied in digital technologies. For example, Chap. 2 investigated the role of dashboards that present information about the COVID-19 pandemic and specifically investigated their ability to track changes over time. Chapter 3 investigated the innovation aspects of the contact tracing application offered by the German government. The application utilized a decentralized tracing ability on a voluntary basis. Chapter 4 presented a concept for a new online platform supporting child development during the pandemic. Since children experience and absorb the wellbeing of their caregivers, digital technologies could be used to leverage and maintain their wellbeing. Hence, research on digital innovation covered all levels of analysis.

Moving forward, IS scholars can investigate further opportunities for digital innovation ideas and concepts. For example, technological advances, such as artificial intelligence and machine learning give rise to novel application domains and new modes of interactions with humans (Rahwan et al. 2019). Artificial intelligence with its increased capability for independent agency might become more readily adopted during a pandemic. As such, digital innovation might offer more advanced process automations than before. The instantiation of intelligent agents, that is, digital objects with rational agent functions (Russell and Norvig 2010), within business processes could help enforcing physical distancing requirements that might be relevant to these processes. While the application domains are plenty, from conversational agents in customer service to predictive algorithms we use in finance, their application in, and implications for, business processes remain unclear. Especially, as we are progressing toward the future, the role and influence of these intelligent agents may change. So does their acceptance or rejection by society. Hence, research on digital innovation can benefit from empirical insights into the decreasing resistance of technological advances resulting from the global pandemic.

The essays on digital transformation included in this book mainly provide conceptual contributions. Given the novelty of the COVID-19 pandemic and its seemingly abrupt appearance, this is not surprising. Digital transformation is a process that involves changes over time. For example, individuals need to identify and develop new techniques and behavior that adapt to the new situation, as our example on the use of digital tools for student learning showed (see Chap. 5). Likewise, organizations need to identify new business processes or adapt their old once in response to the "new normal", as our example on the adaptation of control practices suggested (see Chap. 7). In addition, entire ecosystems have been overwhelmed with attention and identified strategies to cope and leverage this attention, as the case of TikTok suggested (see Chap. 6).

However, as we are moving forward, IS scholars can help society and businesses adapt to the current situation. For example, IS scholars can investigate the increased utilization of digital and virtual learning tools, benefitting from the vast experiences collected in schools and universities worldwide. The experience collected so far during the pandemic suggests that utilization of digital tools for learning will have varying effects. While some benefitted from the digitalization efforts because of prior experience or their own self-interest, others have been stressed due to the additional burden and ended up merely digitizing prior efforts rather than transform learning practices, which often left both students and teachers dissatisfied. Likewise, IS scholars can investigate the impact of policy changes in organizations. While some organizations have been quick to accept remote work from home as a "new normal" workforce situation and extended the arrangements for work from home for a longer period of time or even indefinitely, others tried to get their employees back into the office as soon as possible. Here, IS scholars can help to build knowledge about different forms of digitally enabled individual, organizational, and ecosystem adaptations to COVID-19, in order to better and support the transition toward the "new normal" of the organizational life of workforces, whatever form it may take.

Finally, the essays on digital entrepreneurship included in this book focus on design-oriented and empirical knowledge contributions on an organizational level. Digital entrepreneurship relates to the emergence of new enterprises with the help of digital technology. At the center of such enterprises are novel digital products as market offerings. For example, in Chap. 8, the author investigated the case of a digital venture that pivoted their business idea in the event market from going out to staying inside, via a digital platform. Instead of offering ticket sales to events that were held in event locations, they offered access to livestreams by artists. During the pandemic, retailers were particularly challenged to implement physical distancing guidelines in their supermarkets and grocery stores that customers could easily follow. In Chap. 9, the author designed a prototypical solution for customer flow management in retail environment that could help ensuring physical distancing guidelines within retail stores and supermarkets. In Chap. 10, the author presented a design solution for a restaurant ordering system that digitizes the order process within restaurants, hence protecting the restaurant staff and customers from the risk of potential infections.

As these examples suggest, IS scholars can help tackle future research opportunities in digital entrepreneurship, especially those that concern digital technologies as new market offerings, that is, as outcomes of entrepreneurial ventures (von Briel et al. 2021). For example, the changed situation through a pandemic or other crisis in the entrepreneurial environment can increase the acceptance of more novel and advanced digital technologies. Times of uncertainty and turbulence often generate a surging need for innovative solutions. As such, entrepreneurs that have already researched advanced technologies may receive an unexpected demand increase, while others may be forced to reinvent themselves. At the same time, not all that is new and innovative is useful and fit-for-use in daily contexts. As all our authors of digital entrepreneurship essays have shown, evaluating usefulness and ease of use for customers are essential criteria (beside criteria such as effectiveness to implement certain hygiene measures) to assess the overall success of new digital products.

The three essays also indicate that design could be a particularly useful lens for entrepreneurs to focus on the requirements of the day-to-day use of end users (Berglund et al. 2020). Hence, future research should in particular investigate the short and long-term implications of the pandemic toward new ventures' creation of new digital market offerings. Research questions of interest could involve how new ventures can offer innovative digital solutions that are at the same time adequate in a pandemic. While investigating digital entrepreneurship from a venture's perspective is important (which has been predominant in our authors' essays), we argue that researchers should complement this view by investigating individuals (e.g., Nambisan and Baron 2021) as well as entrepreneurial ecosystems (e.g., Autio et al. 2018). Exemplar open research questions include: Do cognitive perceptions of uncertainty influence digital idea selection of entrepreneurs, or the willingness of customers to try new digital products? Do decisions of venture capitalists about funds and investments in digital ventures shift as a result of COVID-19? And: Does technological expertise in founder teams receive increased attention when making these investment decisions? These are only few examples of where and how IS scholars can help advance the field of digital entrepreneurship in times of a global pandemic.

Future Waves Bring New Challenges

We are writing this conclusion chapter in the middle of a "second wave" of COVID-19 infections in Europe. But this second wave is qualitatively different from the first. While the steep increase in COVID-19 cases was a surprise in February and March, summertime allowed people to be active and outside. Many restaurants increased their outdoor seating capacities and municipalities have been quick to make decisions providing a relevant legal framing. However, since summer, multiple factors have resulted in a recent spike in COVID-19 cases that are expected to continue to increase throughout the winter months in the northern hemisphere. For example, the colder temperature forces people to seek shelter and remain indoors, increasing the chances for the virus to go airborne and spread. Furthermore, physical distancing guidelines have been in place for multiple months, which may have increased the desire to "go back" to whatever was deemed a normal social and cultural life prior to the onset of the pandemic, whether that is feasible or not.

The onset of the second wave and the ongoing evolution of the COVID-19 pandemic now present new and different challenges toward society. While society is now better prepared than before in some aspects, such as the supply of face masks, the treatment of patients, the level of information provision, and acceptance, other aspects, such as the resourcefulness of businesses, the labor market, or the level of psychological burden for many people, are vastly different and in many cases worse than early in 2020.

Hence, within the second wave new challenges will arise, coupled with new needs for digitally enabled responses. For example, previously identified alternatives in order to maintain physical distance, while allowing people to have a social live, may no longer be feasible. During the summer months, many new social alternatives were held outside in the open (e.g., concerts, plays, or other cultural events). Other examples include doing sports outside, rather than in the gym, and dining outside, rather than inside a restaurant. In addition, there are still entire industries that have yet to figure out a way to adapt to the "new normal". While many scientists suggest that COVID-19 will be with us for a couple of years, or even forever, the cinema industry, for example, has yet to come up with a valid new or transformed business model. Potentially, entire industries can fall apart if we do not act. It is this transition of individuals and businesses where IS scholars can contribute and support societal shifts.

While the second wave and thereafter will present undoubtedly challenging times, they also provide new and important avenues for future IS research. Here, we focus on three selected avenues:

1. the surveillance society,
2. the misconception of digital solutions, and
3. the design of practical solutions

First, the COVID-19 pandemic has shown us a *surveillance paradox* (e.g., Leclercq-Vandelannoitte and Aroles 2020). While society took tremendous efforts and precautionary measures have successfully been implemented, they resulted in less negative outcomes. However, the information needed to accomplish and maintain this status, required many people to make sacrifices when it comes to data privacy. Only when we can track the contacts between people, we are able to stop the spread of the disease even further. IS scholars can help examine and resolve these paradoxes in surveillance and privacy concerns. Contact tracing has been, and will continue to be, an ongoing challenge during COVID-19. Governments have developed different solutions for this challenge (Trang et al. 2020). For example, Germany developed an app that works on a decentralized and voluntary basis. Countries such as China mandated the use of centralized tracking software. The effects have varied. China used contact tracing apps effectively to curtail the pandemic, for example, by preventing infected patients or people coming from high risk areas to use public transportation. At the same time, these moves also increased levels of centralized surveillance and in turn anxiety. Similar developments in other countries have prompted scholars to warn about a surveillance society (Riemer et al. 2020). The implicated emotional responses and behaviors are important avenues for future research on the positive and negative effects of the transformative forces of digital solutions.

Second, there has been a development of possible *misconceptions of digital solutions*. The long-term societal effects of offering digital solutions for physical distancing should not lead to a dystopian view where any direct physical social interaction is to be avoided by any means and instead surrogated by technology. Such views have been discussed in infamous science fiction literature such as Isaac Asimov's (1957) novel on a society that has departed from face-to-face "seeing" to only "viewing" each other by means of technology in fear of spread of disease. IS researchers should ask how we can design systems that help us to socially engaged while keeping physical distance in infectious situations instead of digitizing any social context (e.g., Adam et al. 2020). There is evidence to believe that not any social and physical interaction is equally infectious. It could be that selected, few super-spreading events and pandemic hotspots drive infection rates substantially. Digital innovation should not be an end in itself to digitize any social situations. Rather, problem-solution pairs need to be found by IS researchers that match digital innovativeness with positive as well as negative societal impacts at the same time.

Exploring this research avenue may mean that we need to start thinking about fundamental changes in everyday interactions. Sometimes, this means designing processes and interactions without their historicity in mind. For example, how would we design a movie theater if we forgot what they currently or historically look like? Does the concept of a movie theater still make sense in a post-COVID-19 world? If so, how could we accomplish a common experience while maintaining required physical distance within an economically effective business model? For example, in customer service, the use of artificial intelligence (AI) can help maintaining physical distance. This field of AI-human interaction and collaboration provides ample avenues for future research that helps enforcing physical distance. For example, research on conversational agents might help building effective digital customer support. Also, AI can be used in care scenarios to limit the exposure of healthcare workers to infection. For example, a project at Stanford (Pusiol 2020) developed a prototype that can help monitor older adults in order to extend their ability to stay at home alone, rather than being transferred to a nursing home, institutions that have been particularly hit by COVID-19 (Stockman et al. 2020).

In a similar vein, the use of intelligent agents could help manage the spread of misinformation. Intelligent agents could be implemented to intervene on social platforms when misinformation is being spread, as recent implementations from Twitter (Roth and Pickles 2020) and other platforms suggest. Since humans have a tendency to rely on humans rather than on algorithms (Dietvorst et al. 2015), IS scholars could investigate learning and coping processes that individuals employ when engaging with intelligent agents that have been developed and implemented in response to the pandemic.

Third, IS scholars need to help *design practical solutions* for quick responses. Although we can envision many innovative digital solutions for contexts and new problems that the pandemic presents, we are required to keep timeliness and practicability in mind. Solutions will not be widely adopted if user acceptance is low. For example, businesses have been forced to collect data from their customers. When dining at a restaurant, the restaurant is now obligated to hold your contact information. Providing false information to the restaurant also is being fined. However, the management of this process was unspecified, and restaurants developed their own forms and processes, often cumbersome, manual, of poor data quality, and prone to falsification. The processes and solutions proved often to be inadequate for tracing after reporting of an infection. Moreover, the solutions were not sensitive to privacy and data security. Contact details documented on printed paper sheets allowed other visitors of a restaurant access to your private information. Conversely, some businesses invested in digital apps that required customers to enter their contact details first, for example, before being able to see and access the menu, or even before being able to buy a ticket or enter a premise. These solutions potentially allow better control of data quality, but privacy and security issues persist. Moreover, the costs in implementing and maintaining such a process are different from a manual, paper-based process. IS research should investigate these tradeoffs. Based on solid empirical evidence, design-oriented IS research should develop contact-tracing instruments that blend cost-effectiveness with usefulness and other criteria such as privacy and security.

Conclusion

The current pandemic is a stark and vivid demonstration of a research problem that matters (Rai 2017). IS scholars, just like many other scientists in other disciplines, want to help. The pandemic offers both a need and an opportunity for IS research to make the world a better place, a desire many IS scholars feel (Pan and Pee 2020).